NOW, FOR THE FIRST TIME . . .

Everything you need to know to follow the famous Rice Diet in your own home:

- The six phases of the Rice Diet, and which one to choose for the quickest possible weight loss

- A step-by-step guide, including which foods to eat and which ones to avoid

- How long to stay with each phase, and how to maintain your ideal weight once it is reached

- How to develop the mind-set to stay on the program, and how to handle binges

- How to incorporate the diet into your daily life—dining out, entertaining, and coping with the needs of other family members

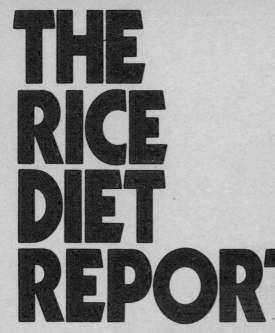

THE RICE DIET REPORT

How I Lost Up to
12 Pounds a Week
on the
World-Famous
Weight-Loss Plan

JUDY MOSCOVITZ

 AVON
PUBLISHERS OF BARD, CAMELOT, DISCUS AND FLARE BOOKS

AVON BOOKS
A division of
The Hearst Corporation
1790 Broadway
New York, New York 10019

First Avon Printing: March 1987

AVON TRADEMARK REG. U.S. PAT. OFF. AND IN OTHER COUNTRIES, MARCA
REGISTRADA, HECHO EN U.S.A.

Printed in the U.S.A.

K-R 10 9 8 7 6 5 4 3 2 1

Some debts can never be repaid.

For giving me life, this book is dedicated to
BESS MOSCOVITZ
my wonderful and supportive mother

and

DR. WALTER KEMPNER
a great healer, an exceptional man.

ACKNOWLEDGMENTS

Every dieter knows how much easier the task is when you have the help, love, and support of others.

I would like to thank the following for being there whenever I needed them:

Irving Silver, the best friend I ever had.

Dr. David Wood of Family Counseling Centers of Northern Virginia, Woodbridge, Virginia—a gifted psychiatrist whose patients are lucky to have him.

The entire medical staff affiliated with the Rice Diet: Dr. Barbara Newborg, Dr. Mercedes Gaffron, Dr. Robert Rosati, Norma Neal, Sharon Ryan, Bob Horn, and all the nurses and technicians. Thank you for being my family away from home.

All my fellow Ricers, both present and past, most particularly Melinda Joy Katzman, Ed Emmerich, Marg Southern, and Jean Lee Brandman.

Non-Ricer friends, guides, and helpers: Randy Norris, Donna Gulick, Sandra "Pappy" Steinberg, Bryan Knight, Rabbi Moshe New, Rose Ronne, Lilah Poncé, and Johanne Johnson.

My sister, Irma Berlin, her children Amy, Andy, and Richard, and my late aunt, Trudy Brensilber.

Dr. Lawrence K. Thompson III, Dr. Verne C. Lanier, Jr., Paul S. Toth, and Karen Bryant, for both information and reformation.

The administration and kitchen staff of the Rice House,

for delicious meals served with kindness and encouragement.

Phyllis Grann, Mort Janklow, Chris Schillig, and Anne Sibbald, for having confidence in my work.

Thanks, too, to my dog Goldie, for constant companionship and for loving me, fat or thin.

CONTENTS

THE RICE DIET REPORT

CHAPTER ONE

Introducing the Greatest Diet in the World

I'VE GOT the greatest diet in the world to pass on to you. At least in *my* opinion, it's the greatest, and believe me, I've tried them all.

It's called the Rice Diet, and it's the only diet that has ever worked for me.

This is my story. In December of 1982, I was a 275-pound ugly mound of flesh, a self-hating woman in constant physical and emotional pain because of my weight.

Nine months later, I had lost 140 pounds, fit easily into a size 4 dress, and had energy and vitality to spare. The Rice Diet had changed not only my appearance, but my entire life!

I expect that many of you will say, "Of course—the Rice Diet. I've heard of that one." Because this is a diet that has been around and has proven itself for over forty-five years. Yet ask most people, even lifelong dieters, what it consists of, and they won't be able to offer you much more than guesses and misinformation.

Many are under the impression that it's a fad diet consisting of nothing but rice, rice, and more rice. Others think it's a diet that permits only rice and fruit.

Only those who have had the opportunity to visit Dr. Walter Kempner's clinic in North Carolina know that "rice and fruit" is simply the first phase of a diet that soon allows you chicken, fish, fruit, vegetables, bread, eggs, hot and cold cereals, etc. In other words, a delicious, nutritious program anyone can follow at home.

1

For over forty-five years, Dr. Kempner, Professor Emeritus at Duke University, has been treating patients at the world-famous Rice House in Durham. Everyone from movie stars to Mafiosi has come here to lose weight.

Until now, the only way to follow this diet was to leave job and family and go to Durham for a lengthy stay. Wonderful if you can do it, of course, but not everyone is in a position to make that choice.

I know how lucky I was to be able to afford the time and the money to go to Durham, and I would like to share my good fortune with those of you who are still battling weight problems but are unable to leave your homes for an extended period of time.

In this book, I will tell you all you need to know to go on the Rice Diet in your own home. For the first time, you will find written down *in detail* all the features of the diet. I'll let you know what foods you can eat and what foods are not allowed; what the six phases of the diet are and which one to choose for the quickest possible weight loss; how long to stay at each phase and how to maintain your loss once you've reached goal.

There is really only one reason I did so well on this diet, and it can be summed up in just one sentence: *I did as I was told.* And if you make the commitment to follow my instructions, I can practically guarantee that you will experience a wonderful transformation in both your body and your life.

WHO CAN BENEFIT FROM THIS DIET?

A quick glance around will tell you that not all dieters are in the same boat. There are major differences in degrees of obesity.

This book is aimed at three categories of dieter:

Group A: *The "Almost-Thins."* Those who would like to lose some weight, but whose eating is basically under control. Say, those with 10 to 30 pounds to lose.

Group B: *The "Betweeners."* Those with a somewhat more substantial weight problem—arbitrarily, from 30 to 80 pounds overweight.

Group C: *The "Constant-Eaters."* Those who are, as I was, massively obese, with 80 to 400 pounds to lose. Many in this group are chronic dieters with a life-long history of dict failure.

I'd like to add that this is also a terrific diet for the person with no weight at all to lose, but who is just not feeling his or her best, not experiencing life with the maximum of power.

In truth, I believe that *everyone*, no matter what his or her weight, could benefit from following the dietary recommendations in this book.

TELLING IT LIKE IT IS

In the forty-five years that the Rice Diet has been around, many other diets have come and gone. You've probably even tried some of them. Most of them did very little good, and some of them were even harmful.

My aim is to furnish you with information that will, in fact, make a real difference for the better in your life. You will lose weight. You will lose weight *quickly*. And you will feel *great*.

This is not one of those understandably popular diet books that tells you you can eat all you want of your favorite foods and still lose weight. Nor will I tell you that calories don't count. If diets like those worked, you wouldn't be reading this book right now.

Diet books aimed at the mass market usually cater to that irrational longing in people—to have it all without paying any price. If it were that easy, who would still be fat?

The plain truth is—and in your heart of hearts, you've known it all along—you *can't* eat all you want, particularly not of your "favorite foods," and still lose weight.

I believe that you must deal with reality if you want to be thin. And the reality is that you cannot eat whatever you want and still be slim. No matter how you try to figure it out, IT CANNOT BE DONE.

You can choose only one option, and you must pay the price for that choice. So far, you have been choosing to eat, and you are paying the price by being fat. And you know what a very high price that is! On the other hand, if you choose to be thin, you will have to give up the kind of eating you've been doing until now.

From time to time I refer to "giving up food," which does not mean giving up *all* food, of course. Nor does it even mean giving up *excess* food, because even that is not good enough for those of us with chronic weight problems (Groups B and C). What I mean is giving up the *wrong* foods—those that harm you and cause a destructive addiction.

Let me reassure you right now: THIS IS NOT REALLY SO BAD. You'll still love what you eat, but you'll be substituting a disciplined, healthy food plan for your current out-of-control, unhealthy eating.

MY WAY OR YOURS?

I personally am totally committed to Dr. Kempner's dietary approach. How could I not be, when it has so profoundly changed my life?

I know the diet inside out, and if you are willing to do exactly what I tell you to, you *will* lose weight. If, on the other hand, you have to change things around and do it *your* way, I can offer no guarantees. I would point out that your way hasn't worked too well in the past, but I can't force you to listen to me. But do be aware that you are making choices, and that your choices will produce certain results.

This is not an easy diet, at least not at first. But you will lose weight quickly and safely on it, and you will feel healthier than you have ever felt in your life. This is not a fad diet. Fad diets leave you depleted and unhealthy—and susceptible to quickly putting the weight back on.

As everyone knows, obesity is a complex problem. No one claims to really understand it, not even the doctors, psychiatrists, and nutritionists who specialize in the field. Certainly, I do not claim to have all the answers. But I sincerely believe that I *do* understand it better than most. After all, I have been there. I know what it's like to be truly obese, what it's like to be somewhat overweight, and what it's like to be really thin.

I know what it's like to diet—how success feels and how repeated failure feels.

I can hand you the same tools I used to lose weight, but you will still have to do the work. It is up to you to use the tools to create something of beauty. Believe me, you'll agree it was well worth the price.

LOSING AND LEARNING

Many overweight people function very well in almost every area of their lives, but when it comes to food and weight, their logic, reason, and determination just don't seem to help. It is my hope to inspire you to choose this diet and to lose the weight you want to lose. But beyond that, I want to help bring you to a pain-free place of sanity about your eating.

I know that some of you will turn immediately to Chapter 7 to get the details of the diet. If you do, I hope that later you'll take the time to read the rest of the book too, because it's the vision and philosophy behind the diet that will make the real difference in getting and keeping your excess weight off.

This is a book that should be read more than once, for losing weight involves more than just dieting. To be truly successful in the long term, the entire process must be seen as a learning experience. Certain behaviors and attitudes will have to be altered permanently.

It is my hope that you will regard this book as a reference work, to be consulted whenever the going gets rough. When troubled by food issues, just open this book anywhere and see if you don't come across some sentence or idea that will help you and see you through.

Remember, your goal must not be just to lose weight, but rather, to put diet, weight, and food problems behind you FOR LIFE.

IMPORTANT NOTE: I was under medical supervision all the time I was on this diet, and you should be too. To protect yourself from potential side effects, frequent medical monitoring is essential. You should consult a physician and get his or her approval before going on this diet, and you should not undertake this or any other dietary therapy without appropriate and ongoing medical supervision.

CHAPTER TWO

Fat Little Judy and How She Grew

I AM THINNER now than I've been since I was seven or eight years old.

I have always had what is euphemistically called "a weight problem." Sometimes I was really obese, sometimes I was just "pleasingly plump." But I was always unhappy about my weight, always going on diets, always counting calories and worrying about my appearance.

I grew up in a loving but somewhat decentralized family. Because we all led very different lives, it was practically impossible for all of us to get together for meals, with the result that we all cooked for ourselves and ate alone.

When I was in elementary school, I would arrive home hungry at three. Instead of settling for a snack, I prepared my supper and ate it right away. This left me feeling hungry again by nine, so I ate still another complete dinner then.

I liked to cook (indeed, I liked anything to do with food), and began preparing my own meals as early as age eight. Naturally, I could only make the simplest of meals, which usually meant throwing a steak or some lamb chops into a pan, then having something sweet and fattening for dessert. I never ate vegetables. This was the early 1950s, when frozen vegetables were unavailable, and vegetables therefore required some time and skill to prepare. I never ate fruit. We were not basically a fruit-eating family, and we rarely had it in the house.

I simply never developed a set of proper eating habits.

Of course, I was always the fattest kid in the class, and I knew all the pain that only a fat kid can know. I never

7

got valentines from boys on Valentine's Day. I was always the last one reluctantly chosen for the teams. And I had to endure the ridicule of the other "normal" kids. (Moscovitz lent itself well to the nickname Mosco-Fats.)

I always felt different from and inferior to the others.

None of this prevented me from continuing to overeat, of course, though I constantly resolved that someday I would "show them all."

But "someday" never came, and I just kept growing fatter. I went from a fat child to a fat adolescent to a fat adult.

Yet, for all my gorging, I never knew what it was like to feel full. I would start a binge feeling hungry, and the next thing I knew, I would feel sick. There was no stopover at "full" on my route. What I did was eat until I felt stuffed and sick, go to my room and lie on the bed on my back until the sick feeling passed—then get up and eat more until I felt sick again.

As an adult, I spent most of my nonworking hours that way. If I wasn't actually eating, I was thinking about food, planning what I was going to eat, reading recipes and cook-books, or wandering through supermarkets. (I used to go *every day,* for the sheer pleasure of being near food.)

To give you an idea of how much I was putting away, I, a single woman, had a monthly food bill of over $600— and that was preinflationary dollars, to boot!

Naturally, I looked terrible and I felt even worse.

I used to get out of breath just turning the pages of a newspaper or lifting a dress over my head. We won't even discuss climbing stairs, which left me panting and heaving for five to ten minutes.

All my joints ached, especially when I first got out of bed in the morning. (I told myself I was getting arthritis.)

I fell asleep at the wheel when driving long distances because my obesity prevented me from getting enough ox-ygen to stay awake. (I told myself I was just tired and needed a good night's sleep.)

I always felt ashamed when I ran into people I knew.

I give a lot of credit to fat people who take good care of

themselves, but I was not one of them. I saw myself as so fat and repulsive that it surely made no difference if my stockings were ripped or my shoes unpolished and run down.

I made no effort at all with my appearance. I just didn't care (although inside I cared and suffered profoundly). It was hard for me to believe that it mattered how I treated my fat and ugly body.

As far as clothes were concerned, I wore whatever fit. *Whatever.* There was no such thing as selecting a style or even a color. I was grateful just to find something that would get around me, even in the "oversize" specialty shops.

It was a life of humiliation, shame, and emotional pain, lived with the constant awareness of what my life *could* be like if only I could lose weight.

Every day—yes, every day—I started a new diet. And almost every day I failed. Oh, occasionally I would say to myself, "To heck with it. If I can't lose weight, I'll just accept myself fat and start living a normal life nonetheless."

But I just couldn't do it. I could never, not even for one minute, accept being fat, never resign myself to spending the rest of my life as a fat person. It just couldn't be.

I had all the paraphernalia related to weight loss: an expensive medical scale, diet books, low-calorie cookbooks, tape measures. There wasn't a diet I didn't try, including some I invented myself.

I constantly made up graphs and charts to use as diet aids. I put a lot of energy into these activities. In fact, I did *anything* to lose weight—except stick to a diet, of course.

Over the years, I tried:

diet doctors, both legitimate ones and quacks

diet pills

hypnosis

fancy spas

spartan fasting farms

liquid protein

herbal wraps

Weight Watchers, TOPS, and Overeaters Anonymous

weight-loss clinics

virtually every diet book ever written

acupuncture

exercise machines

behavior modification therapy, both individual and group

nutritionists

In fact, everything but wiring my teeth shut, stapling my stomach, and intestinal bypass surgery. If there had been anything else available, I'm sure I would have tried that, too!

Yes, I was always trying, but I never did succeed because, at heart, I was unwilling to make the one real choice that had to be made—the choice to give up food. I felt that there had to be some way around it, some way of "having it all." I was unwilling to bite the bullet and just *do it*.

And so I spent many years as a fat person, many unhappy, despairing years. Then, in 1982, something happened that finally propelled me to do something about my weight.

I had left the practice of psychotherapy and started a novel business—a dining-out club for singles—which caught on remarkably well. In the period of one year, I opened ten branches across the United States and Canada.

All the branches did well—but chiefly for other people, not for me. I was a good idea person, but not the best of administrators, and I soon discovered that I was way out of my league. I had neither the business skills necessary to manage such a large enterprise nor the money to hire someone else who could, and the result was that I ended up losing almost everything I had.

The financial losses were difficult enough to accept, but what I really took hard was the personal failure. Except for weight, I had always been successful at everything I tried to do in my life. I was a determined and hardworking person, and I always believed that if I wanted something badly enough, and worked hard for it, it would be mine.

I had truly given this business all that I had. I had worked eighteen hours a day, seven days a week, and without salary, to boot! But no matter how hard I worked, I just wasn't able to pull it off.

For the first time in my life, I had to face the fact that I couldn't necessarily accomplish something, even if I fully put my mind to it. This was the first time in forty years that I came face to face with my own limitations. Incredible as it seemed to me, I *didn't* always know best, and I wasn't always right!

As painful as that lesson was, it was the chief reason I was finally able to really go on a diet.

You see, for the very first time, I was willing to be passive, willing to acknowledge that my way *wasn't* necessarily the best, willing to listen to what someone more experienced told me to do.

By this time, I had ballooned up to 275 pounds, and the end wasn't even in sight. Would I go up past 300 pounds? Past 350, or more? It was *possible*—I was obviously out of control.

My life was such hell that I was finally ready to admit that dieting, unpleasant and difficult as it might be, was surely the lesser evil.

I was so tired of the pain of living a fat life. Tired of the daily "new diets." Tired of trying, tired of failing. Tired of the constant anxiety and desperation. I needed a place of peace. I needed to lay the matter to rest in my life once and for all. I just couldn't take the misery anymore. It had to stop.

For the first time in my life, I was ready to listen to someone tell me what to do. And willing to do it blindly.

Of course, it couldn't be just any adviser, and it couldn't be just any diet.

Like many other people with a weight problem, I had long known about Dr. Kempner and his world-famous Rice Diet. Here was no questionable "diet doctor," but a universally esteemed physician and research scientist with an incredible forty-five-year track record. I knew I could put my faith in him. HE WOULD TELL ME WHAT TO DO, AND I WOULD OBEY.

I resolved to put everything else aside, and make this diet my priority. It was so important to me that I sold everything I owned to get the money I needed to go to Durham for a lengthy stay. I put my house on the market and sold all of my furniture. By the time I was finished, not one book, not one picture, not one record remained. I went to Durham owning only a television set and my dog.

My commitment was total.

I was going to go on the Rice Diet.

I was going to get thin, really thin.

And I was going to work *hard* at putting weight and food problems behind me for life.

CHAPTER THREE

Origin of the Rice Diet

WALTER KEMPNER, PIONEER

DR. WALTER KEMPNER, developer of the Rice Diet, is a brilliant and remarkable man. As a young doctor still in his twenties, he was compared to Pasteur by a noted physician in his native Germany. Now eighty-three, he has devoted his entire life to medical research and to the treatment of his patients.

His work has earned him an enviable reputation among his colleagues and has brought global recognition to Duke University Medical Center, where he has worked and taught for over forty-five years.

His original contributions are the basis of many of today's modern therapies, including:

the restriction of salt in the treatment of hypertension

the move toward low-protein, high-carbohydrate diets

the use of low-cholesterol, low-fat, high-fiber diets

the control of diabetes through diet alone

the use of exercise in the treatment of cardiovascular disease

His publications are too numerous to mention, and his honors include the Gold Medal from the American Heart Association.

Yet this world-renowned man likes to refer to himself simply as a "mechanic." The complicated mechanism that he works on is, of course, the human body.

Dr. Kempner has spent his life investigating the causes and treatment of diseases of the heart, circulatory system, and kidneys, as well as the problems associated with diabetes and high cholesterol levels. Indeed, he first developed the Rice Diet in an effort to remedy the underlying causes of these diseases. It was only by luck and observation that weight loss was discovered to be one of the fringe benefits.

For many years, Dr. Kempner researched the metabolic functions of both healthy and diseased cells. He sought not just to *treat* disease and degeneration, but also to *prevent* them. He knew that if his research proved successful, the entire process of aging could be changed, even delayed.

Thus, it was Dr. Kempner who led the way in the fight against those degenerative diseases responsible for half the annual deaths in the Western world. Prior to his revolutionary treatment, those suffering from the "silent killer" diseases had very little hope. Dr. Kempner's work proved that given the proper dietary treatment, most of these ailments could be improved, and even reversed.

Dr. Kempner's research into vascular changes eventually, and quite logically, led to his interest in obesity. Many serious disorders are complicated and worsened by the presence of excess weight, and it soon became apparent that weight control was an important aspect of total patient care.

LUCK PLAYS A PART

The Rice Diet was first administered to patients in 1939, at Duke University in Durham, North Carolina. Considered revolutionary at the time, the diet uniquely combined a low-salt, high-fiber, low-protein, low-fat, and low-cholesterol regimen.

For the next few years, Dr. Kempner prescribed this diet exclusively as a short-term treatment for critically ill people. It never occurred to him that the diet would become popular. Indeed, he considered it akin to unpalatable medicine and said that the only thing in its favor was that it definitely worked!

It was quite by accident that he discovered the possibilities of the Rice Diet as a mode of long-term treatment.

A local farm woman came to see him with multiple complaints of a serious nature. Dr. Kempner examined her and instructed her to follow the Rice Diet and return in two weeks. However, the patient had never before been exposed to European voice inflections, and she misunderstood Dr. Kempner's German-accented directions. Instead of two *weeks*, she understood him to say to return in two *months*.

Promptly two months to the day later, she returned to his office with a remarkable improvement in virtually all of her complaints.

Dr. Kempner himself was astonished at this outcome. It had been his opinion that the maximum length of time anyone could tolerate the diet was a few days, perhaps a couple of weeks. But this patient's experience indicated that extended use did no harm and that the diet actually increased in effectiveness if administered for a longer period of time.

A few years later, in 1944, Dr. Kempner was invited to speak at the annual meeting of the American Medical Association. He spoke about a sampling of 150 patients who had shown remarkable improvement by following the Rice Diet.

His extraordinary results were documented by a range of photographs, charts, chest films, and electrocardiograms. Nonetheless, because his work diverged dramatically from the mainstream thinking of the day, it was met with skepticism and doubt. One doctor in the audience was even overheard to remark, "Those exhibits must be forgeries!"

The years that followed resulted in a mixed response to Dr. Kempner's work. On the one hand, most medical practitioners did not believe in the importance of proper nutrition in the treatment of degenerative diseases. Basically, they told patients not to avoid any particular foods because what one put in one's mouth was of minimal concern. On the other hand, many physicians began referring sick and obese patients to Dr. Kempner's clinic, and before long, special arrangements had to be made to meet the flood of inquiries.

THE START OF THE RICE HOUSE

At that time, patients were usually hospitalized for the duration of the diet, but it soon became impossible for the hospital to accommodate all those who wished to come.

Dr. Kempner's solution was to provide an alternate facility, a private home, which became known as the Rice House. This clinic-cum-dining hall was started by the wife of one of Dr. Kempner's patients. She had to cook Rice Diet meals for her husband anyway, so she agreed to allow a few additional patients to live in her home and eat their meals there daily. Dr. Kempner and his staff visited patients there each morning, taking their blood pressure and answering questions.

Soon even this additional space wasn't enough, and many other homes in the area began to open their doors to lodgers—all the new "Ricers" who were arriving in Durham in droves.

WHY RICE?

Dr. Kempner is well aware of the hazards of obesity, and the implication of obesity in degenerative diseases and death has led him to treat it in a very scientific manner. His treatment of choice is the health-promoting Rice Diet—not medication, fasting, hospitalization, or surgery.

To avoid the necessity of these radical approaches, he originally sought to devise a formula that would combine medical treatment and proper nutrition in one diet plan. He also wanted to reduce unhealthy food items like salt, fat, and excessive protein to a minimum while including the essential amino acids and fatty acids found in the average North American diet.

It's not surprising that part of his answer lay in rice. This grain is, after all, the staple food of nearly one-half of the world's population. And for the people who subsist on it, as much as 80 to 90 percent of their daily food intake is in the form of rice.

Although North Americans tend to prefer animal protein at meals, most of the rest of the world obtains its required protein from grains. And in the grain family, the protein content of rice surpasses the others in its amino acid structure. Rice, with its eight essential amino acids, permits the cells in our bodies to most efficiently use the protein they receive.

Although in later phases of the Rice Diet reasonable amounts of animal protein are added, the protein in Phase I comes almost entirely from rice. Rice offers a form of protein that is easily assimilated by the body, and your protein equilibrium remains at a normal level even though you are not ingesting much protein at this stage.

North Americans are gradually coming to agree that our traditional diet contains too much protein, especially animal protein. This excess puts a strain on the kidneys and accelerates our metabolic rate, reducing the life span of some cells. An unpleasant consequence—premature aging—can result. Moreover, recent studies indicate that animal protein, particularly beef, can contribute to cancerous conditions—another good reason for deciding to cut down.

Over forty-five years ago, Dr. Kempner realized that the best way to be healthy and lose weight was to cut down on the amount of fat and protein in the diet while emphasizing the role of complex carbohydrates from fruits, vegetables, and grains. In accordance with these findings, Phase I of his diet provides no cholesterol at all and less than five grams of fat. (Note that although rice contains very little absolute fat, it has a high proportion of essential fatty acids, such as linoleic acid.)

The body's chief food need is carbohydrates; indeed, our bodies require three times more carbohydrates than either protein or fat. Thus, carbohydrates furnish about 94 percent of the calories in Phase I, compared with about 50 percent in the average North American diet.

Another difference between the two diets is in the type of carbohydrate ingested. Most Americans eat a substantial amount of their carbohydrate calories in the form of sugar, a *simple* carbohydrate, as opposed to grains, fruits, and vegetables, which are *complex* carbohydrates and better for you.

By the early 1980s, Dr. Kempner's revelations about salt and cholesterol had become common knowledge, and even our beloved protein had come under closer scrutiny. Today, medical professionals routinely advise their patients that life-style changes are necessary in order to conquer obesity, heart attacks, and strokes. We now know that old-time practitioners were wrong in believing that these degenerative diseases could not be stopped. The fact is, in many instances, they can be completely avoided. All that most of us have to do is replace the "normal" foods we eat with the health-producing foods recommended in the Rice Diet.

As one of Dr. Kempner's colleagues wrote, "When we first came to Durham, the medical profession generally was either ignorant of the facts that Dr. Kempner's research and experience had established, or unwilling to accept them. Times have changed, and now the evidence is being slowly accepted everywhere."*

MIRACLES BY THE SCORE

At the Rice House itself, it's impossible to share even one meal without hearing of miraculous transformations in people's lives. Patients who come in unable to walk find themselves, with time, out jogging on the lovely Duke campus. Diabetics who have lost their vision have been known to

* Bernice Krasne. *Bulletin of the Walter Kempner Foundation*, October 1982.

regain their sight. Others, once given only two weeks to live, happily recount their stories twenty or thirty years later.

It's an everyday event for a patient to arrive in Durham taking a dozen or more different pills for his or her ailments—diuretics, tranquilizers, heart or blood pressure medications—and have them decreased or discontinued soon after beginning the diet. Usually the person's blood pressure is dramatically lowered, frequently in only a few days.

And here is another piece of evidence that this diet is both effective and safe: It has been used successfully in the treatment of very young children, who develop and thrive by following its precepts.

I consider myself to be yet another testimonial to the viability and effectiveness of this wonderful diet. I was lucky that I had no medical problems and was just fat. I was what Dr. Kempner calls "a luxury patient." But rest assured that my case is far from unique. Dr. Kempner has thousands and thousands of success stories about patients who have been happily and healthily living on this diet for years.

We, Dr. Kempner's patients, are lucky to have had the opportunity to benefit from his miraculous discoveries. And I am happy to be passing them on to you through this book.

CHAPTER FOUR

"Do It"

WHY, OH, WHY?

A MISUNDERSTANDING OF psychology has led many to believe that before we can do something about a problem, we must know the reasons why the problem exists. I often hear of dieters spending a lot of time and energy trying to understand *why* they overeat. This can have both short-term and long-term application.

Short-term is why you ate *today*. (You were depressed, under stress, premenstrual, or had a rough day at work.)

Long-term is why you have this problem in the first place. (Your mother was overprotective, your father was abusive, you were excessively dependent, etc.)

Frankly, it doesn't matter why you overeat, and it is simply self-indulgence to spend much time or energy exploring the cause. There may, in fact, be psychological work that must be done before some people are healthy enough to make the right choices for themselves, but I do not believe that it consists of unearthing "the reason" why you are overweight.

First of all, I do not believe that there is "a reason," nor do I believe that it can be found. As a psychotherapist, I can tell you that thinking can sometimes be a counterproductive waste of time. Frankly, insight and understanding are fine, but they change nothing. Action does.

Be grateful that it is not really necessary for you to find "the reason" in order to get the job done. Getting the job done consists, quite simply, of doing the job.

I remember a story I heard some fifteen years ago. A young man, about eighteen, suddenly developed spontaneous paralysis in his legs and became totally unable to walk. His worried parents took him from doctor to doctor, from specialist to specialist, but none of them could find anything physiologically wrong with him.

Eventually one doctor recommended that the family consult a famous psychiatrist, and they immediately made an appointment with the great man.

After months of therapy, the psychiatrist finally concluded that the boy was terrified of being inducted into the army. (This took place at the time of the Vietnam War.) He stated that the boy had lost the use of his legs as a psychosomatic reaction to this enormous fear.

The patient agreed with this analysis, and shortly after left his wheelchair and began experimenting with the use of his legs. After several weeks of practice and physiotherapy, he was once again able to walk, even run. Soon he was back to his old self, completely healthy, active, and full of good spirits.

A triumph for psychotherapy, you will say. Proof that knowing the cause of a disorder will cure it posthaste.

Ah, but I'm not finished.

A couple of months after his full recuperation, the boy came home from school to find a letter from Uncle Sam waiting for him. He opened it up and read the "greetings" inside. And fell immediately to the floor, totally (and genuinely) unable to walk!

Knowing the cause of his problem did not alter in the slightest the manifestation of his anxiety. It was interesting, perhaps, but it was not *useful*. It illuminated the issue, but it did not in any way change it.

The same must be said about problems with weight. I think it is undeniably helpful to be in an emotionally healthy state in order to lose weight and stay thin. But being "emotionally healthy" should not be equated with knowing *why* you have an eating problem.

Rather than having to unlock your psychological mysteries before you can lose weight, it is more likely that by eating properly and losing weight, you will come to see an improvement in your psychological state.

In truth, the strength and ability to diet come from actually dieting, not before. Dieting is like anything else you undertake: the more you practice, the more proficient you become. Once you initiate action, it tends to just keep on going.

You don't get ready to diet and then diet. The readiness, the ability to stick with it, comes *as you actually do it*. It simply isn't true that if you do a certain amount of groundwork, you will resolve all the relevant issues and then everything will fall into place. If you believe this, and are waiting for dieting to become easy, I can tell you that you will never be thin.

Unfortunately, it is *never* easy to diet. That is an unpalatable truth, but it *is* the truth. People who like food find it hard to give it up, period. And if you are waiting to be emotionally "ready," I believe you are using your problems as an excuse.

FACING THE HARD TRUTH

You will *always* have a good reason for not dieting, a reason you "had to" eat. Sometimes it will be fatigue, sometimes boredom. Sometimes it will be depression, sometimes stress. Or perhaps you had to entertain someone at a business lunch. Or you had a wedding to go to. From experience, I can assure you that there will always be *something* on your mind or on your agenda.

Face the fact that dieting is sometimes hard and unpleasant. But it is the price you must pay if you want to be thin. There is no alternative.

You are *not* a victim of your desire for food. You are making a choice, and until now, you have been making a harmful choice. I invite you to step back—calmly, objectively. Look at your life one way—fat (and eating whatever you please). Look at it another way—thin (and only occasionally eating the foods that you crave). These are exactly what your choices come down to.

To be thin, you must be single-minded and willing to

pay the price. And that price involves determination, commitment, and sacrifice.

Everyone fat avers that they want to lose weight. The only problem is that they also want to eat. I believe that when you really, unambivalently, want to be thin—*more than you want to eat*—you will lose weight. Quite simply, you will be prepared to make the right choices (most of the time) when choices have to be made. And best of all, over a period of time, you will develop self-mastery, even power.

(If, as you read this book, you find yourself constantly thinking, "Yes, but . . ." I suggest you take a good look at this attitude. It is preventing you from losing weight.)

"DO IT"

I have watched Dr. Kempner talk to hundreds of patients, and many of them have proffered reasons for why they weren't losing weight. Dr. Kempner invariably listens politely, but he always has the same answer to give. He uses only two words: "DO IT."

As he points out, if you're in a bad marriage it is foolhardy to stick around wondering why you married your husband, or why you've stayed with him this long. If you're wise, you take a good look at the situation, conclude, "This is not good for me," and get out.

It's the same with being overweight and your "marriage" to food. Yet people will stay in an overweight situation permanently, directing their energies into ascertaining *why* they overeat.

The genesis of the condition does not matter. You'll never know exactly why, and it wouldn't necessarily help you if you did. There is just one certain fact here. You are living life in a particular state of being—overweight. If you don't like it, and you think it's not good for you, you must decide to get out.

No, it isn't easy. And the one thing that will make it

easier is something you'll rebel at. It is learning to be *passive,* to *do as you're told.*

Acknowledge that you *don't* know best and can benefit from obeying blindly. In truth, by apparently giving up power, you will be gaining true power. By giving up control (*having* to have things the way you like them), you will finally gain control.

Some people can be told what to do. Others can't. If you can't be told what to do, then you obviously can't be on a diet (*any* diet), and you will be overweight for life. It's as simple as that. As one patient remarked, Adam and Eve wouldn't listen to instructions either, and look at what happened to them!

You have already seen the results of doing things *your* way. Are you ready to listen to what someone else tells you to do? To follow unquestioningly, even though you don't like the advice? Even though you don't agree with it, and can't necessarily understand it?

Following instructions can be hard, but if you are convinced that the source knows something that can help you (and Dr. Kempner is an impeccable source), then try, just this once, to do as you're told. Remember, you don't have to like it, agree with it, or understand it. You just have to DO IT.

A Lesson from Fido

The process is not unlike training a dog.

For his own well-being, a dog must learn to obey certain commands—"Stay," "Heel," and "Come," to name just a few. This is not because you, his master, are capricious, and not because you want to deprive him of his freedom and pleasures. No, it is because you know more than the dog. You know about the dangers of traffic and of eating garbage off the ground. Your insistence that he obey you is completely for his own good. It is, quite simply, a matter of life and death for your pet.

The dog does not have to understand the reasoning behind your command. And he certainly does not have to like it or agree with it. He just has to DO IT. He has to listen and obey without question. The choice, for him as for you, is a shorter, more painful life versus a longer and healthier life.

As a psychotherapist, I made an extra effort both to understand Dr. Kempner's philosophy and to like it. (Why not? If I could learn to like it, obviously it would be that much easier to stick with.)

But both understanding it and liking it came *after* I started to do it. I didn't demand full understanding and approval *before* I would do it. I knew, after all, that it definitely worked. First and foremost, I wanted to get the weight off. The fine points could come later.

THE PERFECT DIET

You too will lose weight, if you follow instructions. Over the years, more than 20,000 patients have come to the Rice House to be on this diet, and in every single case, patients who followed instructions have lost weight.

I admit that it's difficult to do something you don't really enjoy, but the reality is, if you keep searching for the perfect diet—the painless one that allows you to eat all that you want of your favorite foods while the weight pours off—you will never be thin. Just acknowledge that you are facing a difficult and sometimes unpleasant task, and go ahead and DO IT.

The Rice Diet is not a fad diet. This is a plan that has proven itself again and again for close to fifty years, a diet developed by a world-renowned physician with a long and successful track record.

With this plan, you will discover that each day you diet not only contributes to your weight loss, but also improves your metabolic functioning and increases your ability to stay on the diet. You'll find that each time you take one step forward, it becomes easier and easier to take the next step.

Stopping an addiction is an ongoing process. You have to learn not only new lessons, but the same lessons over and over again. Yes, a flash of insight can help you through a bad time, but it cannot lay the problem to rest once and for all. However, with continued dedication and commitment to your goal, you *will* get the results you want.

The Rice Diet is well designed to help you attain that goal. It introduces you to—and teaches you to like—food in its delicious natural state. It retrains your palate. It helps you cope with limitations, frustrations, and discipline. It truly changes your life, both physically and psychologically.

CHAPTER FIVE

What Should My Goal Weight Be?

IT MAY SURPRISE you to see a whole chapter devoted to the subject of goal weights. Most diet books offer a one-page chart and nothing more.

I believe that the goal you set for yourself will have a determining effect on how successful you are at keeping your lost weight off permanently. The topic thus merits a discussion in depth.

The standard formula for arriving at a woman's goal weight is to allot 100 pounds for the first five feet of height, then add five pounds for every inch over that. For men, it's 106 pounds for the first five feet, and six pounds for every inch thereafter.

RICE DIET GOALS

Dr. Kempner's goal weights are significantly lower than those usually recommended by insurance companies, which use the standard formula. For instance, I am 5'4¾" tall, and according to the standard formula, I should weigh 125 pounds. Dr. Kempner's goal for me is 111 pounds, fully dressed, including shoes. A low figure, to be sure, but his reasons are compelling, and I believe he is right.

The following table gives you Dr. Kempner's recommended goal weights for both men and women. Since these weights include clothing, you should deduct approximately two pounds if you normally weigh yourself undressed. Heights given are without shoes.

For every quarter inch over a given height, women should add one pound and men a pound and one-quarter.

Thus a woman 5'3½" tall should weigh 106 pounds, and a man 5'11¾" should weigh 159.

I know, I know. I can hear you screaming from here. "What? Is he kidding???!!! I haven't weighed that little since the day I was born!"

But stop just a moment and think of the usual weights of beauty queens. Those lovelies who win the Miss America and Miss Universe pageants are always at weights similar to these, if not lower. And far from being scrawny or undernourished, they are considered the ultimate in shapeliness and appeal. There is no need to fear that weighing so little will make you unattractive and gaunt.

I'll note that Dr. Kempner makes no distinction between varieties of body type. He does not give different goal weights for those with small, medium, and large frames.

And rightly so. After all, how can you *know* how large your bones are until you're at your sparest and can really see them clearly? When I weighed 275 pounds, people were always telling me that I had big bones. How could they even hazard a guess about what those deeply shrouded bones were like? Today, these same people tell me how tiny I am!

Nor can you count on that old standby of encircling your wrist with your fingers. If you're overweight, your wrists *also* have an extra layer or two of fat.

Women

Height	Weight Should Be* (pounds)	Height	Weight Should Be* (pounds)
4'11"	91	5'6"	117
5'	94	5'7"	122
5'1"	97	5'8"	127
5'2"	100	5'9"	132
5'3"	104	5'10"	137
5'4"	108	5'11"	142
5'5"	112	6'	147

* when fully dressed

Men

Height	Weight Should Be* (pounds)	Height	Weight Should Be* (pounds)
5'2"	110	5'10"	150
5'3"	115	5'11"	155
5'4"	120	6'	160
5'5"	125	6'1"	165
5'6"	130	6'2"	170
5'7"	135	6'3"	175
5'8"	140	6'4"	180
5'9"	145	6'5"	185

* when fully dressed

Certainly Dr. Kempner's goal weights are low, but that doesn't mean that he's missing the mark. He advances the following reasons for recommending these goals.

The Safety Factor

A long time before you reach Dr. Kempner's goal weight, you are going to be thin. Visually, you may even be thin *enough*. The important question, however, isn't "Am I attractive?" but rather, "Am I *safe*?" Safe from regaining the weight you've taken off.

Dr. Kempner believes that the treatment for excess weight should be 100 percent, as complete as the treatment for cancer or tuberculosis. Otherwise, he cautions, relapses can occur.

He makes the comparison between a cancerous tumor and fat. Surely it is preferable to remove 100 percent of the cancerous cells than to remove only 98 percent and thus risk a recurrence of the disease. Our disease is somewhat similar to a life-threatening cancer. If it doesn't actually kill you (and often it does), it effectively destroys much of your pleasure in life.

Another way to look at it is to point out that the flight distance from Paris to New York is 3000 miles. You may be *most* of the way there when you've gone 2999 miles, but you'd still be unwise to disembark at that point! Wait until you're safely on the ground before getting out of the plane.

In other words, if you don't get rid of *all* your excess weight, you place yourself in danger of gaining it back. Dr. Kempner contends that those who reach the goal weights he has determined and stay there for two years need never fear putting their weight back on again. Surely this kind of security is worth going that extra mile!

People with food problems are always going to be subject to the occasional binge. Unless you're really thin, a few bad days can turn you from slender to stocky—and scared. Once at goal, however, while those excess pounds may not be welcome, they're certainly not threatening. Your stomach might be briefly distended, but you're still thin . . . thin and *safe*.

You're better off dieting two weeks too long than one day too short. The price you might have to pay is simply too high.

Your Best Weight

Obviously, you are losing weight because you want to look good. But how can you know at what weight you'll look your best until you have the opportunity of actually seeing yourself there? Getting to goal is not just a question of becoming thinner. It's also a valuable way of gathering information that you need.

I looked good at 125 pounds, and I could easily have stopped there. But then how would I have known how much *better* I'd look and feel at 119? To date, 119 is the closest I've come to Dr. Kempner's goal, and I'm longing to know what the steps from 118 to 111 will bring. At this low a weight, every pound makes such a difference!

I believe you should go all the way to goal, then decide, based on evidence, how much you want to weigh. Compare the experience to moving to a new city. If you're considering several cities, how can you decide wisely without visiting them all? Only by having been in each one can you know which is the best place for you. It's the very same process when deciding on your best weight.

It's entirely possible that once at goal, you will conclude that it's too low for you. But you will be deciding from the perspective of knowledge, and not guesswork.

It's important to fully experience each of those last few pounds. As the weight drops off, observe how you look and how you feel. How does your body move? How do you look in clothes? If you decide you're too thin, I know you won't have any trouble putting a few pounds back on! But you will have ascertained by actually *being* there your very best weight. Any other approach is like picking a number out of a hat.

Self-Mastery

What motivates most people to lose weight is the desire to look good. But vanity, though a strong force, can propel you just so far. It can take you to the point of being slim and looking attractive, but once it is satisfied, many dieters stop there.

I believe it is a mistake to make "looking good" your only goal. Though unquestionably of value, it is not enough for long-term results. You should continue dieting until you're safe—not just from a weight gain, but from the pain of having been overweight.

Once vanity is satisfied, only the desire to put the pain permanently behind you can push you the rest of the way to goal. Being at a *really* low weight effectively removes you from the fray.

I see getting to goal as acquiring self-mastery, the final victory of your will over your desires. It is conquering your unwise yearning to overeat and laying to rest your inappropriate love of food. Personal power lies in controlling your passions. Self-mastery means that your appetites don't control *you*.

Peace of Mind

Getting to Dr. Kempner's goal can help you put food and weight problems behind you for life. Essentially, it involves a rejection of the importance of food, because only if you are willing to make food (on the whole) unimportant to you can you hope to achieve such a very low weight.

Is it worth it? For me, yes. It is one less thing to worry about in life. But I leave it to you, and point out the following. Getting to Dr. Kempner's goal means *never* having to be self-conscious about your weight. Not having to worry about holding in your stomach, or how you sit or stand. Knowing you look graceful and attractive *any* way you move.

No passing comment, no real or imagined slight, can ever get to you or hurt you; you will be invulnerable on the subject of weight. At Dr. Kempner's goal weight, you'll *know* you are really and truly thin—and that knowledge can give you enormous confidence and strength.

Not Convinced?

If none of the above has managed to make an impact, perhaps the following point will. Dr. Kempner states that once you reach his goal weight, your "furnace burns better." In other words, your metabolism burns food more efficiently, permitting you to eat more without gaining weight. If nothing else motivates you, surely *this* will do the trick!

ONE MORE WORD

When you're selecting a doctor to help you with your program, be sure to choose one with whose goal weight you agree. I strongly suggest that you discuss this issue during your very first visit. A shared goal is part of the process of working together toward one end.

It helped me very much to have Dr. Kempner's collaboration while I was losing weight. It spurred me to continue because I wanted to please him and earn his respect. Investigate a little, and you'll find a responsive physician, too.

WEIGHING YOURSELF

You should weigh yourself daily, before you eat or drink anything and at approximately the same time each day. Then enter your weight on a chart like the one below. This will help you keep track of how you're doing and how far you still have to go.

Sample Daily Weight Chart

Date	Weight	Loss Per Day	Loss from Start	To Go to 125
May 12	148	—	—	23
May 13	144½	—3½	—3½	19½
May 14	143	—1½	—5	18
May 15	141¾	—1¼	—6¼	16¾

A blank form follows for your use. Enter your own goal weight on the empty line in the last column.

My Daily Weight Chart

Date	Weight	Loss Per Day	Loss from Start	To Go to _____

MEASUREMENTS

Weight is only a part of the picture, of course. Your measurements are another indication of how well you are doing.

Before embarking on the diet, take a measuring tape and jot down how many inches you are around the bust or chest, waist, abdomen, hips, thighs, knees, calves, and upper arms.

Measure again each time you have lost ten pounds.

Use the following chart to keep track of your progress.

My Measurement Chart

Date					
Weight					
Bust/Chest					
Waist					
Abdomen					
Hips					
Left Thigh					
Right Thigh					
Left Knee					
Right Knee					
Left Calf					
Right Calf					
Left Arm					
Right Arm					

PHOTOGRAPHS

As I mentioned elsewhere, I think you would profit from keeping a photographic record of your progress. Have a friend take your picture before you start the diet and after every ten pounds or so you lose. Take several shots, showing front, back, and side views.

Date each picture and write on the back how much you weighed when it was taken. You might also want to jot down what size clothes you were wearing at the time.

CHAPTER SIX

The Durham/Rice House Experience

THIS CHAPTER has two purposes. One is to inform you, the reader, about life in what is sometimes called "Diet City, U.S.A." The other is to serve as a thank-you note—I'd even call it a love letter—to Durham, North Carolina, where I spent three very happy and productive years.

Durham is part of an area known as "The Triangle," which consists of Durham, Raleigh (the state capital), and the charming university town of Chapel Hill. I am not the only one who loves it here. Rand McNally's *Places Rated Almanac* this year ranked the Triangle as the third "most livable" area in the entire United States, calling it, quite rightly, "a genteel place to live."

The state of North Carolina is green, friendly, and hospitable. The city of Durham (population 105,000) offers exceptional educational, recreational, and medical facilities in an unusually restful and attractive environment. You'll find no traffic jams here, no highrises, and no big-city pressures. It is easy to feel at peace here very soon.

Before Dr. Kempner's arrival in 1934, Durham was best known as a tobacco town. Now diet clinics are listed among its top revenue-producing industries. Indeed, Durham has become known as the best place in America for the reputable treatment of obesity. There are about 500 dieters here at any one time, and a Chamber of Commerce study indicates that dieters spend over $40 million a year in the town.

There are few local industries that are not affected by the diet population. Real estate owners rent hotel rooms, apartments, and rooms in private houses to dieters. Restaurants cater to their needs by offering calorie-restricted and salt-free meals. All clothing stores feature large-size departments, and sports shops sell thousands of pedometers and pairs of athletic shoes each year.

The local population is, by now, familiar with the sight of massively obese strangers walking their streets, and this casual acceptance is part of what makes the Durham experience so comfortable and happy. Believe me, there are very few places in America where the 200-pound-plus person can feel unembarrassed and at ease!

Most of the dieters who end up in Durham are considerably overweight, by anyone's standards. An excess of 40 pounds is about the minimum that you'll find, and there are many who come with 200 to 400 pounds to lose. One occasionally hears stories about 700-pound-plus patients being brought to town in the back of a pickup truck, unable to fit into the more conventional modes of transportation. Durham can be seen as the last resort for those who have tried virtually everything else in their quest to lose weight.

The fame and the distinguished medical reputation of the Rice Diet program have attracted patients from all over the world, and you'll hear an assortment of international accents at meals. About half of the patients are here for medical reasons; the other half comes strictly to lose weight.

Their professions are diverse, but most are leaders in their fields. It is common to encounter a supreme court justice over breakfast or share a table with a movie star at lunch. In particular, you'll find many, many physicians and members of physicians' families. Some are here to study and observe; most come to experience the benefits of the Rice Diet for themselves.

As you would expect with a program demanding a residency of one or more months, most of the people who come here are wealthy enough to be able to afford to leave their jobs for a lengthy period of time. There is usually a string of Cadillacs and Mercedes outside the door, and sweatsuits with diamonds are, for some, every-day gear.

Not everyone is in that fortunate position, of course; there are many, like me, who sold everything they owned to purchase this opportunity for themselves.

A DAY AT THE RICE'S

A typical day on the Rice Diet begins in the morning when the "Ricers" come to check in.

We put on our name tags, weigh ourselves (those over 300 pounds use a special scale in the back room), then lie down to have our blood pressure taken. This is the time for us to discuss whatever problems or questions we may have.

Crossing the hall, we then enter the dining room for breakfast. This is a plain, unadorned room (tablecloths once a week only, on Sunday), an example of what one patient calls the "reverse snobbery" of the Rice House. There are no frills in the decor, or in the food prepara-tion. Dr. Kempner believes it is unnecessary to make eating a wonderful experience. We *already* find it too delightful!

Each of the seven tables in the dining room has six chairs around it, and dieters sit down wherever they choose. Since some patients are finishing their meals and leaving while others are just arriving, you have a shifting assortment of dining companions along with your meals.

A great deal of attention is paid to food at the table. Some wisely limit this topic to the foods available at the Rice House ("Is the soup good today?"). Others cannot resist going on about the foods they wish they were eat-ing—the ones responsible for bringing them to Durham in the first place.

Because I feel strongly that painting wonderful pictures of things you can't have is a form of torture, I avoided the tables where food talk ran rampant.

Time between meals is completely unstructured, and

most dieters use these hours to engage in exercise programs. Some limit themselves to walking; others join the Y or the sundry spa programs available in town. Shopping is always a popular "sport," especially for those in need of new, smaller wardrobes!

Evenings are usually spent in socializing of one form or another. The local discos offer "Dieters' Nights" (known by habitués as "The Crisco Disco" because of the amount of lard present!). Those on the diet programs congregate and dance, many for the first time in their lives. Other dieters prefer to go to movies at night or to Broadway plays performed by national touring companies.

Duke University offers many free classical concerts, as well as occasional lectures by such literary luminaries as John Irving, Bernard Malamud, and Tom Stoppard. Indeed, for such a small city, Durham has something for everyone in its lineup of activities.

Entertaining at home is very popular, too, and friendly groups of dieters often get together for an evening of board games and conversation. Needless to say, no refreshments are served!

COSTS

How much does it cost to come to the Rice House?

Well, the medical program itself is not too expensive. In fact, it's a fraction of what one would pay at a luxurious spa. It's only $150 a week for round-the-clock medical attention, and what's more, the price hasn't been raised in over twenty-five years! Dr. Kempner and his staff are motivated by scientific and humanitarian concerns, not by money. In fact, Dr. Kempner has repeatedly turned down millions offered by those wanting to turn his program into "big business."

Apart from the weekly medical costs, there are, of course, other expenses to consider. Food at the Rice House is $9 per day, which includes all three meals as well as service. Extra tipping is optional, and certainly not expected. Living expenses—rent, clothes, transportation, entertainment, and the ever-popular "miscellaneous"—also add up. In all, one would find it difficult to get by on less than $1500 to $2000 a month.

The initial medical workup, administered before you are permitted to enter the program, is considered one of the finest in the country. It is extremely thorough, and costs anywhere from $800 to $1500, depending on how many tests you need. Generally speaking, the younger you are, the fewer tests are required. A second battery of tests is administered when you leave, the cost being in the $200 to $300 range.

Some of the above expenses are covered by private medical plans; others are not. If you are considering a sojourn in Durham, you will want to check this out beforehand.

ONGOING MEDICAL SUPERVISION

The incoming routine for all new and returning patients entails the taking of a detailed history, a less thorough examination, and a full range of tests, X rays, and chemical analyses.

Thereafter, patients are required to submit urine samples twice a week, and these are tested for sodium, chloride, protein, albumin, sugar, and acetone. About every three weeks, blood chemistry is checked, and for some patients an occasional extra test, X ray, or consultation is required. Charts are kept on an ongoing basis. These monitor the condition and progress of each individual dieter.

Though your initial workup is done at Duke Hospital, where all Rice Diet doctors are affiliated, subsequent patient-doctor meetings usually take place at the Rice House, where the entire medical staff makes a daily visit. In fact, a full-facility clinic is set up in the living room of the Rice House each and every morning, seven days a week. Dr. Kempner and his staff arrive sometime before seven o'clock and remain available until nine-thirty or ten for anyone who wants to sit down and talk to them.

The Rice House medical staff has been together for many years. It is a close-knit group of interesting and individualistic professionals who have devoted their entire lives to the treatment of their patients. Their genuine interest and concern are unmistakable, and they quickly become like a family away from home for most of their patients. They are always on call should you need to speak to them, and they never seem to get discouraged or give up on anyone under their care.

ALAS, A POOR PROGNOSIS

I consider myself very lucky that Dr. Kempner took a personal interest in me from the day I first arrived. As he says, he "put his nickel on me" at the very beginning. Needless to say, his concern helped me a lot!

I've sometimes wondered how he knew that I was one of those who were really going to do it. But after a while, I too was able to distinguish the serious dieters from the rest. Or, more accurately, it soon became obvious which "dieters" stood little chance. They were the ones who:

talked constantly about food

planned what they were going to eat as soon as they left Durham

jotted down where to get the best Danish in Denver, just in case they ever happened to be in that city

sat out on the front porch barking when I brought scraps to my dog

went to the supermarket daily to see, touch, and smell food

kept junk food in their apartments "to prove I can resist temptation" or "just in case I feel weak"

offered to buy other dieters illegal foods, in order to have the pleasure of watching someone eat

spent long hours working on jigsaw puzzles of pizzas

gnawed on the already gnawed-on chicken bones left on the table by other dieters who had finished eating

Then, of course, there was the still-legendary group of four dieters who one night, on a binge that took them to almost every restaurant in town, spent a total of $800 on food. This did not include liquor, and it is a particularly prodigious feat in Durham, where a four-course dinner may be bought for under ten dollars in even the best restaurants in town!

I also don't have too much hope for the woman who has lost and gained 100 pounds six times—so far.

REEDUCATION, NOT INTROSPECTION

In general, I would say that the ones who continue nurturing their attachment to food are the ones least likely to attain success with this program.

Those who recognize that what is being offered is not just a diet but a program of *gradual reeducation* are the ones who profit most.

There are some who complain that there is no psychological component to the program, and, in fact, there is no *formal* psychological adjunct. It is my professional view, however, that the program itself is brilliantly formulated so as to provide an intense, ongoing, *informal* experience in group therapy. In this unthreatening but stimulating setting, it is impossible to come away without having learned a great deal about yourself and your problems.

Those who request it (or who are perceived to need it) are referred to outside psychotherapists, but for the majority, Dr. Kempner's mix of diet, exercise, and "motivational enhancement" is more than enough to do the trick.

SHOULD I CONSIDER GOING TO DURHAM?

The Durham/Rice House environment is, in many ways, ideal for losing weight. After all, you are there for that one purpose. Your focus is on yourself, and you are removed from the pressures of work, family, and home. You have nothing to concentrate on but your own schedule and your needs. For many, it is the only time in their lives that they have put themselves first. Your time is spent most agreeably: joining your new friends at meals, shopping, walking, exercising, getting a massage.

But there is something to be said for doing it at home, too.

At home, you have access to the people and things that are familiar to you. You have the support of those who love you and the distractions of your usual activities and your work.

You have the opportunity of working closely with your own personal physician.

You do not have to attend to onerous details (like finding an apartment, acquiring furniture, etc.) while at the same time working at staying on a diet.

You are not living far from home in a town where you don't know a soul. You are therefore less likely to be lonely.

Of course, only you can judge where you're likely to do best.

The truth is that comparisons serve little purpose. One

fact is true, no matter where you are: THE RICE DIET WORKS IF YOU FOLLOW IT EXACTLY. The next section provides all the information you will need to know should you decide you'd like to try it at home.

CHAPTER SEVEN

The Rice Diet: Phase I

THIS DIET has been famous for more than forty-five years under the name "The Rice Diet." Which is a pity, in a way, because the name can be misleading, even discouraging, to those considering going on it.

It's all too easy to dismiss the diet by saying, "Oh, I couldn't stand eating only rice day in and day out." And I couldn't agree with you more! But how would a diet that allows chicken, fish, fruit, vegetables (including potatoes), soups, salad, bread, and eggs suit you? Well, the Rice Diet offers all of that, and more! *Eventually.* And therein lies the beauty of this plan.

The diet has a total of six *graduated* phases. In Phase I you will lose the most weight in the shortest period of time. Phase VI is maintenance, and three different slim-forever plans are offered for the three different categories of dieter mentioned in Chapter 1. Phases II through V are developmental phases, in which a selection of new foods is gradually introduced, step by step, in keeping with the needs and requirements of the individual dieter.

As for rice—well, if you like it, you will find it a delicious, nutritious, and filling addition to your meals. But if you're not partial to it, you'll be happy to know you can follow this diet 100 percent with only a minimal intake of rice.

There are all kinds of pluses to this program.

- You lose weight quickly and safely.

- You are allowed a wide variety of delicious and healthy foods.

46

- The foods permitted can be readily adapted to a great number of interesting recipes.

- You learn to like food in its natural state.

- The diet promotes new, healthy eating habits while working to correct your old, destructive ways of eating.

- There is no need to purchase special foods, and all the foods required are reasonable and affordable. In fact, many high-priced "diet" foods, such as lobster and shrimp, are not even allowed on the diet.

- You will find that far from becoming harder, the diet becomes easier and easier with the passage of time.

- The diet program encourages regular exercise, but not overexertion.

- You do not need to purchase special exercise equipment of any kind.

- You will feel your health improving day by day.

- The diet aims at altering your life-style *permanently*. It thus offers far more than just a temporary weight loss.

But in order to avail yourself of all of the above benefits, you must follow the diet *exactly as it is written*. Even small additions or changes can ruin the effect. Years of observation have shown that those who insist on modifying the regimen do not get the same remarkable and permanent results as those who adhere to it 100 percent.

Please remember that no one should apply this or any radical dietary therapy without appropriate medical care. If you think you would like to follow this diet, it is important that you consult a doctor first, and then on an ongoing basis.

Your doctor has probably heard of Dr. Kempner and his famous Rice Diet, and I believe he or she will agree that, properly supervised, this is a healthy and well-balanced program designed to bring about quick and beneficial weight loss for great numbers of dieters.

PHASE I FOR
SUPER-QUICK WEIGHT LOSS

Phase I of the Rice Diet is different from the average American diet in a number of ways. It offers twice as much carbohydrate, one-quarter of the protein, and a small fraction (less than one-twentieth) of the fat.

Indeed, Phase I of the Rice Diet could easily be regarded as the real test of character! It consists of nothing but rice (and its equivalents) and fruit, with selected beverages.

Yes, this sounds monotonous, but at least it is simple! There are no difficult instructions to follow, and the food is tasty, inexpensive, and easy to prepare. Best of all, you lose weight so quickly that you'll feel motivated to see it through!

I personally know of two cases (both women who weighed over 400 pounds) in which losses of 40 and 50 pounds were recorded in two weeks!

Of course, you can hardly call that typical, but the typical weight losses aren't so bad, either. I myself lost 19½ pounds in the first two weeks (12 pounds the first week, 7½ the second), and I would say that the average weight loss in a two-week period is from 15 to 25 pounds.

One of the best things about the diet is that after only a few days your appetite largely disappears. This is partly due to the blandness of the food you are eating, partly because of the restriction of salt, spices, and protein. The monotony itself works in your favor to curb your appetite, and you shouldn't be surprised if after only a few days you're pushing your plate away, unfinished!

The following menu outlines exactly what you are allowed to eat during Phase I.

Every day is the same in term of quantities, but the selection of fruits and rice equivalents is up to you. You may choose any items you want from the lists of permitted foods that begin on page 51.

Breakfast   1 fruit
Any noncaloric beverage

Lunch   2 fruits
1 portion of cooked rice or its equivalent
Any noncaloric beverage

Dinner   2 fruits
1 portion of cooked rice or its equivalent
Any noncaloric beverage

Typical Menu Plans

Average daily menus might look something like these:

——————————— DAY 1 ———————————

Breakfast   1 orange
Decaffeinated coffee

Lunch   1 cup fresh strawberries
1 cup canned pears, unsweetened
¾ cup hot rice
Lemonade

Dinner   Pureed cream of rice with
1 banana
1 fresh apple
Herb tea

——————————— DAY 2 ———————————

Breakfast   1 cup sweetened grapefruit segments with 2 tbs. juice
Decaffeinated coffee

Lunch	¾ cup shredded wheat mixed with
	1 cup unsweetened applesauce and
	⅓ cup raisins
	Tea

Dinner	1 cup unsweetened canned peaches poured
	over
	1½ cups puffed wheat
	¼ cup dried apples
	Coffee

—————————————— DAY 3 ——————————————

Breakfast	½ grapefruit sweetened with sodium-free
	sweetener
	Coffee

Lunch	1½ cups puffed rice mixed with
	1 cup unsweetened fresh fruit salad
	1 slice watermelon
	Limeade

Dinner	¾ cup cooked cream of rice mixed with
	4 prunes and
	1 cup fresh blueberries
	Iced tea

The above menus are simply examples; they are not required eating. You should feel free to select whichever fruits and rice equivalents you prefer. You can vary your choices, or you may stick with your favorites meal after meal. PICK FRUITS THAT YOU ENJOY.

RICE AND ITS EQUIVALENTS

You are permitted to eat one portion of any of the following at lunch and at dinner. This means a maximum of fourteen times per week (seven lunches, seven suppers). Even if you're not partial to it, you should have some form of rice at least six times a week during this phase, to ensure adequate nutrition.

Note: No canned or frozen "rice dinners" are permitted, nor are you allowed commercially packaged rice mixes, etc.

Rice

You are allowed *any* kind of rice, as long as it contains no sodium. (Some brands of instant rice contain sodium, so check labels carefully.) Your "permitted" list includes white rice, brown rice, parboiled rice, long-grain rice, Basmati rice, instant rice, etc. No wild rice, which is not really rice.

The rice should be placed in a strainer and thoroughly rinsed before cooking. Cook according to package direction but be sure to *omit salt*. Use plain water and rice only.

Rice may be eaten hot or cold.

QUANTITY: ¾ cup of cooked rice per meal.

Puffed Rice

Use the plain, unsweetened kind, with nothing else added. It is available in many supermarkets and in health food stores. Check the label carefully to make sure that the package contains nothing but puffed rice.

QUANTITY: Up to a maximum of 1½ cups per meal.

Puffed Wheat

The plain, unsweetened kind, with nothing else added—it's available in many supermarkets and in health food stores. Check the label carefully to make sure that the package contains nothing but puffed wheat.

QUANTITY: Up to a maximum of 1½ cups per meal

Shredded Wheat

Again, the plain, unsweetened kind with nothing added.

The only brand I know of that contains nothing but the wheat itself is Nabisco. Found in most supermarkets. You may use either the whole "biscuit" or the spoon-size shredded wheat.

QUANTITY: *Whole,* one biscuit per meal.
                Spoon-size, ⅔ cup (about 16 little squares) per meal.

Cream of Rice

Prepare according to package directions, with water only. Available in most supermarkets.

QUANTITY: ¾ cup of cooked cereal per meal.

FRUITS

All fruits are permitted, with the exception of dates, avocados, and tomatoes. Dr. Kempner recommends that you peel all fruit before eating.

Fruits may be eaten fresh, canned, dried, or frozen. Canned fruit may be in its own juice or water-packed (called "unsweetened" in the listing) or in sugar syrup ("sweetened"), as long as the can contains nothing but fruit, water, and white sugar.

Fruit juices of any kind may be substituted for whole fruit, if desired. One cup of juice is equal to one fruit.

If you select juices, those freshly made are your best bet, unless the canned or frozen products contain no form of sodium. Check labels carefully. Fruit "drinks" and fruit-"flavored" drinks are not permitted.

The following quantities are considered to be "one fruit."

apple
     fresh   1 medium
     dried   ¼ cup
applesauce

unsweetened	1 cup
sweetened	½ cup
apricots	
fresh	3 average
canned, sweetened	½ cup
canned, unsweetened	1 cup
dried	¼ cup
banana*	1 medium
blackberries (including dewberries, boysenberries, and youngberries)	
fresh	1 cup
canned, unsweetened	1 cup
canned, sweetened	½ cup
blueberries	
fresh	1 cup
canned, unsweetened	1 cup
canned, sweetened	½ cup
frozen, sweetened	¼ cup
cantaloupe	½ average
casaba melon	¼ average
cherries	
fresh	1 cup
canned, sweetened	½ cup
canned, unsweetened	1 cup
dried	¼ cup
cranberries	
sauce	¼ cup
jellied	¼ cup
currants	¼ cup
figs	
fresh	2 medium or large, 3 small
dried	2 medium or large, 3 small

* Dried banana chips are not allowed because of the other ingredients used in processing them.

fruit cocktail
    canned, sweetened   ½ cup
    canned, unsweetened   1 cup
fruit salad
    canned, sweetened   ½ cup
    canned, unsweetened   1 cup
    fresh, with 2 tsp. sugar   ½ cup
    fresh, with no-cal
       sweetener   1 cup
grapes (all kinds)   1 cup
grapefruit
    fresh   ½
    sections, canned,
       sweetened   1 cup
guava   2 medium
honeydew melon   ⅕
kumquat   1
lemon   as desired
lime   as desired
mandarin orange
    fresh   2 small
    canned, sweetened   ½ cup
    canned, unsweetened   1 cup
mango   1 medium
melon balls, frozen,
   sweetened   ¾ cup
nectarine   1 medium
orange   1 medium
papaya   1 cup cubes
peach
    fresh   1 medium or
                       large
    canned, sweetened   ½ cup
    canned, unsweetened   1 cup
    dried   ¼ cup

pear
    fresh   1 medium
    canned, sweetened   ½ cup
    canned, unsweetened   1 cup
    dried   ¼ cup
persimmon   1 average
pomegranate   1 average
pineapple
    fresh   ¼
    dried   ¼ cup
pineapple slices, chunks,
  tidbits, and crushed
    canned, sweetened   ½ cup
    canned, unsweetened   1 cup
plums
    fresh   2 small, 1
                                            medium or
                                            large
    canned, sweetened   ½ cup
    canned, unsweetened   1 cup
prunes
    dried   4
    stewed   4
raisins   ⅓ cup (one
                                            1½-oz. pkg.)
raspberries
    fresh   1 cup
    frozen, sweetened   ¼ cup
    frozen, unsweetened   ½ cup
    canned, sweetened   ½ cup
    canned, unsweetened   1 cup
rhubarb, fresh   1 cup after
                                            cooking
strawberries
    fresh   1 cup
    frozen, sweetened   ¼ cup
    frozen, unsweetened   ½ cup
    canned, sweetened   ½ cup
    canned, unsweetened   1 cup

tangelo	1 average
tangerine	1 average
watermelon	1 slice, 10" diameter, 1" thick (about 2 cups)

CANNED FRUITS, BOTH WATER- AND SUGAR-PACK, MAY BE
SERVED WITH 2 TBS. OF JUICE PER SERVING.

Although it is not a requirement, you would be wise to
choose at least one Vitamin C fruit a day. These include
citrus fruits (orange, grapefruit, tangelo, tangerine), melons (cantaloupe, casaba, honeydew, and watermelon), and
strawberries.

The following recipes can give variety to your meals.
Each recipe makes one serving but may be increased pro-
portionately if you wish to make several servings at one
time.

STEWED PRUNES

Use 4 prunes. Cover with boiling water and let stand for a
few minutes to soften. Drain off the water and add 2 tbs.
canned prune juice.

PRUNE "ICE CREAM"

Remove pits from stewed prunes. Puree in blender with 2
tbs. prune juice. Freeze and serve.

FRUIT "ICE CREAM"

Any canned fruit makes a delicious sherbetlike dessert.
Place the permitted portion in a blender, along with 2 tbs.
of its juice. Puree, freeze, and serve, slightly softened.
Pears, peaches, and apricots are very tasty this way.

BANANA POPS

Crush shredded wheat. Cut a banana into 1-inch-thick slices and roll in shredded wheat. Stick a toothpick in each piece. Serve as is, or freeze and serve frozen. Shredded wheat can be sweetened with sodium-free sweetener if desired.

FRUIT COBBLER

Place one of your allotted fruits in a baking dish. (This recipe is particularly good with apples, peaches, or berries.) Add $1/6$ cup of raisins (which equals half a fruit). Drizzle on 2 tbs. frozen orange juice concentrate (another half a fruit). Sprinkle with your allotment of cream of rice, dry. Cover with foil and bake in a 350° oven for 45 minutes. Uncover and continue baking until the top is brown. Serve warm or cold.

APPLE PUDDING

Cut an apple into pieces and boil in 1 cup pineapple juice until soft. Pour over crushed shredded wheat and mix. Serve warm.

STUFFED BAKED APPLES

For each apple, mash half a banana with 2 tbs. raisins. Core the apple and stuff with banana-raisin mixture. Bake for half an hour in a 350° oven. Serve warm or cold. Pineapple chunks make an interesting substitute for the raisins. (Use an amount equal to half a fruit.)

STRAWBERRY-RHUBARB COMPOTE

Boil 1 cup strawberries together with 1 cup rhubarb. Add a couple of tablespoons of water if the mixture sticks to the pot. When soft (about 15 minutes), remove from stove and add sodium-free sweetener to taste. Serve warm or cold. Delicious over puffed wheat or puffed rice.

You may find it strange at first to eat dry cereal without milk, but there are many delicious combinations (like the compote above) that you can pour over it to "wet" the cereal and enhance the taste. All canned fruits with their syrup are delightful, and fresh fruits (with the exception of citrus fruits) are also good choices.

Some combinations I have tried and like over dry cereals are the following:

banana and raisins

applesauce and pineapple chunks

applesauce and raisins

banana and canned peaches

½ banana, berries, and ½ cup orange juice

Another hint for making the cereal less dry is to add your fruits the night before, then let the mixture "set" in the refrigerator overnight. Shredded wheat is particularly tasty this way—it becomes moist, cakelike, and truly delicious.

BLENDED RICE

Blended rice is a very popular dish at the Rice House. It is sweet and dessertlike, and whips up into a plentiful and filling quantity.

To make it, simply whip up the fruit of your choice (including 2 tbs. syrup if you are using canned fruit) with your allotted portion of cream of rice. Add sweetener to taste. Use either a blender or a food processor, or mash up your fruit with a fork. Virtually all fruits except citrus fruits lend themselves well to this treatment.

BEVERAGES

In all likelihood, you will not be very thirsty after the first few days, since you will be eliminating all salt and spices from your diet. But be sure to have a minimum of 24 ounces of fluid a day (three 8-ounce glasses) because this is a high-fiber diet.

Do not have more than a maximum of 40 ounces of fluid per day (five 8-ounce glasses), except in warmer weather, when this may have to be increased.

It makes no difference if you have your beverages at meals or between meals. Do whichever you prefer.

If you choose herb teas, be sure to read the labels to make sure they contain no sodium or sodium compounds.

Caloric Beverages

One cup of any unsweetened fruit juice can be substituted for one fruit. However, you might be wise to *eat* your fruit, rather than drink it, so that you will feel more full and satisfied. This will also ensure that you are getting adequate amounts of fiber in your diet.

Permissible juices are:

apple juice

apricot nectar

cran-apple juice

cranberry-grape juice

cranberry juice cocktail

grapefruit juice

grape juice (purple or white)

orange juice

peach nectar

pineapple juice

prune juice

NO TOMATO OR MIXED VEGETABLE JUICES ARE ALLOWED.

Noncaloric Beverages

Permissible noncaloric beverages are:

water

decaffeinated coffee

tea (regular, decaffeinated, or herb)

lemonade or limeade (made at home with juice, water, and sodium-free sweetener only)

SPICES AND CONDIMENTS

There are two basic tastes that people enjoy: salty and sweet. This diet meets those tastes with the use of *fresh lemon juice* (for a salty tang) and *sodium-free sweetener* (e.g., Equal or Revco drugstores' brand). NO OTHER SPICES, HERBS, OR CONDIMENTS ARE ALLOWED. NONE. Do not use bottled or canned lemon juice. Do not use salt substitutes. Do not use fresh or dried herbs.

This is so important that I have devoted entire sections of this chapter to the restriction of salt and spices. I urge you to read them carefully. Your willingness to adhere to this one restriction will make all the difference in the world to your success on this diet.

SALT

You are likely to find that the most unusual aspect of this diet is its virtually complete elimination of salt. YOU CANNOT AT ANY TIME, IN ANY PHASE, ADD SALT TO ANYTHING THAT YOU EAT.

I'd be willing to bet that there are very few of you who do not routinely add salt to food. And I'd also be willing to bet that few of you love salt a fraction as much as *I* did before I went on this diet.

I grew up with a mother whose formula for salting foods was, "Keep adding salt till you're positive that you've put in too much—then add a little more." And I did!

I salted *everything*. And when I say "everything," I include even such shocking items as anchovy pizza and bacon! When I cooked a steak, I would salt it before cooking, salt it again on the plate, then cut a bit and salt each individual forkful before I ate it!

This amounted to a virtual addiction. I literally could not tolerate food without lots of salt on it. If I went to a wedding and a waitress came around with a platter of hors d'oeuvres, they were almost tasteless to me until I whipped the salt shaker out of my purse and "spiced them up" before eating. Yes, I carried a salt shaker in my purse on such occasions! I also had a salt shaker in my office, and still another in the glove compartment of my car. Heaven forbid I should be caught in a food situation without salt on hand because I simply could not imagine enjoying any food without it.

I tell you this so you can know that no matter how much you love salt on your food, if someone like *me* can learn to eat food without it—and even enjoy it!—then surely so can you!

The salt restriction in the Rice Diet is more all-encompassing than in any other diet I've encountered. That means some caution is in order.

Salt is a vital compound; we need it to live. It is therefore crucial to maintain the proper balance of salt to fluids in our bodies. It is not usually a problem getting all the sodium we need because it is present in so many foods we consume. In fact, sodium is so readily available that no "daily requirement" for it has ever been established.

Most dieters adapt readily to the restriction of salt, but in some instances, electrolyte disturbances (sodium and potassium imbalances in the blood and changes in its acidity or alkalinity) can occur, and if ignored, the consequences can be severe. Please be sure to remain under constant medical supervision.

Salt Abuse

Studies indicate that the human body needs less than one-quarter of a gram (one-sixteenth of a teaspoon) of sodium per day. This is a very small amount, and many of us use far more than our bodies require, often twenty to thirty times more than we need.

Unfortunately, too much sodium can produce painful and dangerous consequences. For example, it can contribute to a wide range of illnesses, from hypertension to premenstrual distress. Salt is not the harmless condiment we would fondly like it to be. The fact is, it can do us a great deal of harm.

One of the problems is that the more salt we eat, the more we seem to want, with the result that salt becomes almost an addiction. We purchase foods that contain salt, salt them again before cooking, then again at the table. Many people salt their food even before tasting it, and some of us can hardly taste foods without layering a substantial coating of salt on it first. We develop a tolerance for salt that makes us crave more. When you consider that most baby foods contain added salt, it is not surprising that so many people develop this destructive habit early in life.

Though salt is admittedly a tasty compound, it is a mistake to think that it *improves* the taste of food. In truth, it *disguises* it, and creates in us a dulled sense of taste.

Salt abuse leads us to believe we *have* to have salt—at the very least, on *some* foods. (Have you ever contemplated eating an egg or a tomato without salt?) This leads to the formation of a salt habit that can be difficult to break.

Most people do not start paying attention to their salt

intake until an actual problem arises (high blood pressure, for example), and by then it's often too late.

Though initially it may seem difficult to stop, salting foods is actually one of the easiest habits to break. Of course, food will taste bland at first, but there are no withdrawal symptoms, and after a reasonable period of time most people find that they don't miss the salt taste at all.

Salt and Other Sodium Compounds in the Rice Diet

IT IS A CRUCIAL PART OF THIS DIET THAT YOU NEVER ADD SALT TO ANY OF YOUR FOOD. Nor can you eat foods that have salt (or any other form of sodium) previously added to them in processing. This eliminates virtually all canned foods, and many frozen foods as well.

Cutting down on sodium is not just a matter of not adding table salt to the foods you eat. Unfortunately, we also have to watch out for the various sodium compounds added to canned and processed foods. *Any* sodium compound causes the same problems as table salt, and the numbers of these compounds are legion. Let me list just a few of the sodium compounds that are commonly added to our foods:

sodium alginate	sodium gluconate
sodium benzoate	sodium lactate
sodium bicarbonate	sodium mono-fluorophosphate
sodium caseinate	sodium nitrate
sodium citrate	sodium phosphate
sodium erythorbate	sodium propionate
	sodium saccharine

Sometimes the word "sodium" is hidden somewhere else in the name, as in:

calcium disodium	disodium inosinate

disodium guanylate   disodium phosphate

monosodium glutamate (the popular MSG)

And these are just a few!

In fact, sodium is so ubiquitous, it is virtually impossible to know just how much of it we're taking in daily. But you can be sure that the more processed foods you eat, the more sodium you're absorbing.

Another source of "hidden" sodium is medication, both prescription and over-the-counter. I suggest you read carefully the list of ingredients in your medications, and if they contain any form of sodium, ask your doctor if there is a sodium-free equivalent you can take.

Envelopes and stamps contain sodium in their glue too, so you'd be well advised to start using a sponge, instead of your tongue, to seal them.

Benefits of Salt Restriction

On Phase I of this diet, your sodium intake will be less than 20 milligrams a day. As you proceed through the phases, it increases somewhat but still remains less than 60 to 100 milligrams per day.

Because sodium is so stringently restricted, most people who follow the diet notice that they're hardly ever thirsty. Fluid intake decreases noticeably. (You will be happy to hear that this is not one of those diets that forces you to drink eight or more glasses of water a day!)

Because you are taking in almost no salt, you will find that you no longer retain water, for any reason whatsoever. You will quickly feel less bloated and will soon appear much less puffy. In fact, you should see a visible difference within just a few days.

The elimination of salt has still another positive effect: it reduces your appetite. Spicy foods tend to stimulate your appetite and make you want more.

Sodium in Water

One last word about sodium. Many municipalities have an excessive amount of sodium in their tap water. If the concentration of sodium in the tap water in your area is greater than 20 milligrams per liter, you would be wise to use distilled water instead.

A list of the sodium content in the water supplies of some major American cities can be found in the Appendix at the back of this book. If your city is not listed, a call to the water supply department of your city government should quickly secure the answer for you. Another possible source of this information is your local chapter of the American Heart Association.

SPICES

NO SPICES, HERBS, OR CONDIMENTS OF ANY SORT ARE PERMITTED ON THIS DIET, WITH THE EXCEPTIONS OF FRESH LEMON JUICE AND SODIUM-FREE SWEETENER.

Dr. Kempner points out the illogic of trying to lose weight while working to make food delicious. Obviously it makes the task even harder if you have to do without foods that tempt and delight you! You are far wiser to eat foods that meet your basic nutritional needs but don't incite you to eat more than you should.

At the Rice House, I observed that this was one of the hardest restrictions for most dieters to obey. Although no spices are available at the Rice House itself, many dieters bring in their own and add them at the table.

I too went through a "disobedient" phase, when I came in carrying my cache of condiments. However, I soon saw that I was doing myself a disservice. Instead of feeling satisfied at the end of a meal, my taste buds had been aroused, and I sat there in a bad and resentful mood, wanting more. After only one week of this, I threw out my spices, and I haven't touched them since. I have found that lemon juice and sweetener meet my needs well enough and don't pique my appetite.

I have heard many dieters say, "Hey, there are no calories in these spices. I don't understand why I can't have them if I want to." Well, you don't *have* to understand why you can't have them, nor do you have to like or agree with the rule. But if you're wise, you'll follow it nonetheless.

If your food has to be "just right"—just the way you like it—you are helping to maintain your attachment to food, instead of working at distancing yourself from it. In the long run, this choice will be crucial. I believe that making your food "tasty" will make the diet *harder* for you, not easier.

I cannot stress too strongly my conviction that this rule should be followed. DO NOT ADD SALT TO YOUR FOOD. DO NOT ADD SPICES, HERBS, OR CONDIMENTS—NOT EVEN THE "SODIUM-FREE" KIND. USE FRESH LEMON JUICE AND SODIUM-FREE SWEETENER *ONLY*.

I'm pleading with you—DO IT!

VITAMINS

One multivitamin pill should be taken daily.

At the Rice House, we take ours at breakfast, and the kind we are given are the standard, over-the-counter multivitamins available at any drugstore.

Recently I have begun substituting a "vegetarian formula" multivitamin and mineral pill that I buy at a health food store. These pills contain extra Vitamin B-12, which is lacking in a vegetarian diet, and since I personally choose to eat very little animal protein, I prefer them. Until you get to Phase IV of the diet (which adds animal protein), these pills might not be a bad choice for you, too.

BRAN

Rice and fruit provide you with a good deal of fiber, and it should not be necessary to supplement your daily intake with bran. However, if you are eating only white rice, you may occasionally find yourself constipated. If so, feel free to add a couple of teaspoons of miller's bran to your meals. This is a very inexpensive item found at any health food store.

CALCIUM

Americans today are hearing more and more about the dangers of osteoporosis, especially for women over forty. Insufficient calcium could be a factor in this problem.

Since the Rice Diet prohibits dairy products in phases I through V, some women dieters may wish to take calcium supplements on a regular basis. The latest findings recommend that premenopausal women might take 800 to 1000 milligrams per day, while postmenopausal women might take 1400 milligrams.

Most over-the-counter calcium supplements available in drugstores contain sodium, and I therefore recommend that you investigate the supplements available in health food stores. Read the labels to make sure the one you choose contains no sodium or sodium compounds.

DIZZINESS

The restriction of sodium in your diet usually causes a beneficial drop in blood pressure, which occasionally causes a slight feeling of light-headedness when you change position. This is nothing to worry about, and it passes in a couple of seconds. To prevent it completely, get up slowly from lying to sitting and from sitting to standing.

Note that this problem can be exacerbated if you are taking tranquilizers, sedatives, or sleeping pills. But you probably shouldn't be using these medications anyhow—

most are very quickly dispensed with by dieters at the Rice House. The diet and exercise program makes them feel so good, they don't need them!

FATIGUE

It is not unusual to feel a little tired the first week or so after starting the diet, especially toward the middle of the afternoon.

This quickly passes and is no cause for concern. Soon you'll be waking up full of energy and raring to go. Most will find that this vitality stays with them all day. In fact, living with zest soon becomes a delightful and permanent new way of life!

HOW LONG SHOULD I STAY ON PHASE I OF THE RICE DIET?

The answer to this question is easy! Assuming your doctor okays it, you should stay on this phase *just as long as you can,* and as long as you're obtaining rewarding results.

At the Rice House, patients stay on each phase as long as they (and their systems) can tolerate it. I know very few who have stayed on Phase I for less than two weeks, and I have seen many eat nothing but fruit and rice for four to five months.

You will be losing so quickly on this phase (and your appetite will be so reduced) that you will feel very encouraged to stick with it. As the doctors say, "If your stocks are doing so well, why sell them *now?*" Of course, this is more than just your decision, and your doctor will let you know if your body is reaching the stage of requiring other foods.

After a few days of rice and fruit, you will be surprised to find that when you think of cheating (and you will!), you will be longing for *vegetables,* not for sweet or salty junk foods. The Rice Diet will have already started its astonishing work in altering your palate and restructuring your tastes.

It is important that you then be ready for Phase II, even before you go on it. Read ahead, and have the necessary ingredients on hand in the house. I even suggest that you cook up a pot of tomato sauce and freeze it, so that you will not have any cause to break the diet when you're surfeited with rice and fruit until you just can't stand it one minute more. To my mind, anyone healthy should be able to make it through a minimum of three weeks. You'll be thrilled with the results, and if I may make a little pun, your efforts to stay on this phase as long as possible will bear you much fruit!

MISCELLANEOUS TIPS

- Since fruit is the mainstay of this phase of the diet, you should buy the freshest, finest, juiciest fruit you can find. You will be spending very little money on food and should therefore feel free to treat yourself to something special if you want, like strawberries out of season or imported papayas. Always buy fruit that *appeals* to you.
- Don't keep more food in the house than you will need. Food on hand knows your name and will keep calling to you until eventually you answer. If other members of the household require foods that you're not allowed, consider locking them up in a cupboard to which everyone but you has the key.
- Rice and fruit are very easy to take to work, and they make a tasty and filling lunch. Perhaps you can go on the diet using the "buddy system" with a colleague who also wants to lose some weight.
- I suggest that before you start the diet, you take photographs of yourself from all angles. Take more photos as you go along, to slowly familiarize yourself with the new you. Sometimes it's hard for us to know what we look like to the rest of the world, and looking in a

mirror doesn't really tell us. It's especially hard to incorporate a *new* view of ourselves into our old concept of how we look. I'm sure you can imagine how hard it was for me to adjust to the new Judy who appeared as I lost weight. I looked literally nothing like the person who first arrived in Durham. I personally found ongoing photographs invaluable in incorporating a new self-image as I got thin.

- Forget about the upcoming phases of this diet and concentrate fully on where you are now. I remember one patient asking Dr. Kempner on her very first day if she could eventually eat dairy products. His wise answer was, "Avoid the use of the word 'eventually.' Just think of the next five minutes, and handle *them*." And he's right. Get through *today* and worry about tomorrow later.

- For a sense of discipline and control, before sitting down to a meal write down what you plan to eat on a 3″ × 5″ notepad. Mark down every single item, even coffee and water. Then set out your meal and stick to what you have written.

- Although you are allowed to eat fruits in sugar syrup, you get twice as much fruit and no sugar at all if you select water-pack fruit or fruit in its own juice. I believe this choice will gradually help you lick your attachment to sugar, and I therefore recommend that you consider aiming in this direction.

- I used to drink so much water with meals (remember my salt intake?) that my uncle once put a goldfish bowl full of water beside my plate, instead of a glass! Naturally, I was always running to the bathroom, including waking up several times a night to go. During the first few days of this diet, when you are drastically altering your eating (and salting) habits, you can expect to urinate very frequently. This soon passes, and you can expect nights of unbroken rest and a general feeling of well-being.

- Eat at regular hours. Your body will get used to being fed at certain times and no others. Pick a one-and-a-half-hour period for each meal, and slot your meals in at those times.

At the Rice House, meals are served early. Breakfast is available from 7:30 to 9:30, lunch from 11:15 to 12:45, and dinner from 4:15 to 5:45. When I cook for myself, I move these times forward a bit to conform to usual North American mealtimes. But I make sure to eat my meals within my chosen time periods without fail.

- VERY, VERY IMPORTANT: Do not be a martyr on this diet. You should feel comfortable eating anything that you're allowed. If you like bananas, then eat bananas. Don't tell yourself you'll save calories by having half a grapefruit instead. This diet is difficult enough without making yourself feel even more deprived. It is important that you do whatever you can to help yourself stay on it as long as possible.

  Dieting is usually equated with suffering, but that need not be the case. Remember that it is something you are doing *for* yourself, not *to* yourself.

  Although, of course, calories do count, this is a very low-calorie diet, no matter what fruits you choose to eat, so why deprive yourself just to save 30 calories or so? Believe me, you will lose weight quickly anyway, even if you eat bananas or dried fruit at every single meal.

- If you're particularly hungry at a given meal, feel free to select the biggest fruit you can find. True, "one fruit" means an *average* apple, orange, or pear, but if you're feeling deprived and fragile, picking a really big one will make a difference of only 20 or 30 calories. If it prevents you from feeling resentful, and maybe even breaking the diet, it's well worth making that choice.

  It is important to be obedient on this diet, but it is equally important to be *reasonable*. A few extra fruit or rice calories aren't going to hurt you or harm your progress on the diet.

- If you're not particularly hungry at a given meal and don't finish all your rice and fruit, don't feel that you can eat it later. When a meal is finished, it is finished— you don't get to store up your food or your calories. Eat as much as you want of what you're allowed at meals, and *that's it*. The unsuccessful dieters at the Rice House were those who carted out leftover fruit "for later." Get out of the habit of eating between meals, even if the daily calorie content would be the same. Remember, it is lifetime eating patterns that you are struggling to change and improve.

- If you are not very hungry at a given meal, don't feel you have to finish all the food you're allowed. Just eat as much as you want. You can even skip a meal entirely if you're sure you'll be able to go without food until the next scheduled meal. I personally never ate breakfast because I tend not to be hungry first thing in the morning, and skipping breakfast hasn't hurt me one bit.

- Of course, cheating is not allowed. But that doesn't mean that it never happens. Sometimes you need something extra—a treat—to get you through a rough spot. I allowed myself to chew gum whenever I wanted—both sugar-free and regular. I particularly like fruit-flavored bubble gum, which gives you a burst of sweet flavor when that is what you most desire.

I sometimes go for weeks on end without any gum at all; other times I'll eat as many as three or four packages in one day. Gum has about 20 calories per piece, so some caution is advised. But if this is the worst cheating you ever do, believe me, you're well ahead of the game.

I know of other "cheaters" who allow themselves the occasional no-sodium diet drink. If you try this, be sure to read labels carefully, as most soft drinks, even diet drinks, contain hefty portions of sodium.

Moreover, the packaging of drinks can be misleading. Some are marked "salt-free," and they *are*, but they're not *sodium*-free. Others say they're "low-sodium," and compared with regular soft drinks, they are. But, unfortunately, the sodium content is still too high to be acceptable on this diet.

The only brand I know of that makes an acceptable

low-sodium drink is Diet-Rite. Perrier water is okay too, as are distilled water and seltzer water with less than 10 milligrams of sodium.

There will be other acceptable "cheats" later on in this program, but for the time being, you should limit yourself to just these two—and infrequently.

CHAPTER EIGHT

Phases II
Through V:
Development

YOU'VE NOW been on Phase I of the Rice Diet for at least a few weeks, and you're feeling that it's time to move on.

Perhaps that phrasing is not quite precise. If you're like most Ricers, by now you're probably thinking, "One more day of this diet and I'll *scream!*" Only if you're at *that* point, and your doctor okays it, are you ready to switch to Phase II!

By now, you have probably experienced a range of emotions, from moroseness ("I can't bear this. I just *hate* dieting.") to euphoria ("I lost another two pounds today! I feel great!").

Physically, you've ranged from slightly tired (on occasion) to ultra-energetic (most of the time).

Despite the occasional rough spot, you're delighted with the results and proud of yourself for seeing the diet through. In truth, you probably didn't even find it that hard.

But you've had it with fruit and rice. You don't care if you never see them again in your life. Even your beloved bananas have lost their charm. Surprisingly, what you're really yearning for now is a plateful of vegetables.

It is interesting to observe that if plain vegetables had been offered to you before you started this diet, you would probably have turned up your nose at them, or wanted them served salted, spiced, or sauced. Now, however, even plain boiled broccoli can make your mouth water. As for a baked potato . . .

This diet works well *physically* because it provides, quite simply, the proper fuel for the human machine, the food intended by nature to sustain life in man. It works well *psychologically* because of the way the diet is constructed. Instead of feeling *deprived* by such a simple and bland diet, by working continuously toward the addition of new food groups your palate is gradually "cleansed" and altered, so that even the plainest foods come to taste delicious.

A few weeks ago, you were craving the processed, chemical-laden foods that were destroying your appearance and your health. Today, after a few weeks on rice and fruit, all you really want is a hearty helping of vegetables!

Phases II through V take you from the basic rice and fruit plan right through to Maintenance. Each phase adds a new selection of foods, until you are on what is called at the Rice House "Open Diet"—a varied selection of tasty foods, built into a nutritious and well-balanced regimen.

It is important to stay on each phase just as long as you can, moving to the next only when you're almost at the end of your rope. That way, you will fully appreciate each new food group as you add it. For many of you, you'll be savoring the *true* taste of food for the first time in your lives—and loving it!

Each time you enter a new phase, please reread the guidelines and restrictions outlined in Phase I, as they apply to *all* phases of the diet.

Remember: NO SALT OR SPICES AT ANY TIME.

PHASE II: TOMATOES AND TOMATO SAUCE

Phase II is a transitional phase that will lead to the reintroduction of vegetables into your diet.

Now, in addition to the foods permitted in Phase I, you may select one of the following as one of your food items both at lunch and at dinner.

—————— RICE DIET TOMATO SAUCE ——————

For each serving, use 2 ripe, peeled tomatoes, ¼ whole green pepper, cut into pieces, and ¼ medium onion, diced. Boil together over medium heat until onions and green pepper are soft. If you like a thinner sauce, you may add a little water. If you like your sauce thicker, keep on boiling it until it boils down in quantity and thickens.

Optional: Experiment with fresh lemon juice and sodium-free sweetener for a "sweet n sour" version of this sauce.

—————————— TOMATO SALAD ——————————

Use 2 peeled tomatoes per serving. Add ¼ green pepper, cut into strips, and ¼ medium onion, sliced. Serve with lemon wedges, if desired.

Phase II permits the addition of these two items only. No canned tomato sauce, tomato paste, tomato juice, or mixed vegetable juice is allowed. Canned tomatoes without salt may be substituted for fresh, if desired. Use 2 whole tomatoes per portion.

Typical Menu Plan

Breakfast remains the same as in Phase I.

You may now substitute one of the Phase II items for

one fruit, both at lunch and at dinner. You are still permitted only three items per meal at these times; however, a little more variety is now possible.

A typical day during Phase II might be:

Breakfast   1 fruit
Any noncaloric beverage

Lunch   Tomato sauce
1 portion of rice
1 fruit
Any noncaloric beverage

Dinner   Tomato salad with green peppers and onions
Shredded wheat
1 fruit
Any noncaloric beverage

If you have been following Phase I of the Rice Diet perfectly, you can expect your first taste of tomato to be nothing short of divine. I have eaten in some of the finest restaurants in the world, and I can tell you that I never tasted a better dish than my first bowl of tomato sauce served at the Rice House!

Miscellaneous Tips

• My first "cheat" took place after two weeks on rice and fruit. Craving vegetables, I went out to a fast-food salad bar and put away five plates of mushrooms in a row. Far from getting smaller, each plate was more loaded than the one before. By the time I got to my fifth plate, you could almost ski down the huge hill of mushrooms! And at that point, I was adding dressing, too. I knew for sure I was ready to move on to the next phase! I therefore repeat my advice to be *ready* for Phase II. Have some tomatoes, green peppers, and onions on hand in the house, and cook up and freeze several portions of tomato sauce.

- Every once in a while, a new Ricer expresses some concern for his or her health in considering going on such a stringent diet. I always find it amusing that people embarking on such a healthy regimen are concerned about their well-being—especially considering the junk and chemicals they've been putting into their mouths until now! Believe me, compared with the way you've been eating, this diet can only make you feel better and healthier, never worse.

- Don't be concerned if you don't have a bowel movement every day. It is not necessary. Trust your body to regulate itself.

- How are you doing without salt and spices? Remember that spices stimulate your appetite. (In fact, that's one of the chief reasons for their existence.) As for salt, not only does it affect us physically, as noted, but a recent study at Northwestern University indicates that it also affects us emotionally, making us feel edgy and distressed.

- Most Ricers pour their tomato sauce over their rice, for a tasty, Italian-style dish. You might also try cutting your tomatoes into wedges and alternating them with onions and green peppers on skewers. Bake or broil them until crispy or soft, as you prefer.

PHASE III: VEGETABLES

From this point on, most vegetables can be included in your diet plan. However, some "diet regulars," such as celery, spinach, and watercress, are excluded because of their high sodium content. Legumes, dried peas, and dried beans are also not included in this phase.

It is preferable to select *fresh* vegetables, because of their fiber content and because the majority of their nutrients are intact. Frozen vegetables are permitted, as long as no salt at all has been added to them. There was a time when most frozen vegetables were completely unsalted. Lately I have noticed that many packages are marked "lightly salted."

Unfortunately, this means that they cannot be included on the diet. I hope that this book will cause manufacturers to reconsider and give us the plain, frozen vegetables that we need.

No regular canned vegetables are allowed, as they are very high in sodium. But canned vegetables that are *completely sodium-free* (not just *low*-sodium) may be used, though their fiber content is very poor and their nutrients have been greatly reduced in processing. Though permissible, I cannot go so far as to say they are *recommended*. They should be regarded as a poor third choice.

Read labels carefully when buying any processed foods. Buy products that contain only the vegetable itself or only the vegetable and water. Remember, even small traces of sodium are enough to ruin the quick-weight-loss effects of this diet.

The following quantities are considered to be "one vegetable." Portions given are for cooked vegetables. Only the vegetables listed may be eaten. Note that a handful of vegetables have been marked "once weekly." These optional vegetables have a higher than average sodium content, so if you choose to include them, limit yourself to only one portion of any *one* of them each week.

artichoke, fresh	1 medium, once weekly
asparagus	
fresh, ½" diameter at	
base	15 to 20 spears
frozen	½ package
canned, no-sodium	½ can
bamboo shoots	8 oz.
beans, green, yellow or wax	
fresh	1 to 1½ cups
frozen, regular,	
or French cut	1 to 1½ cups
canned, no-sodium	1 to 1½ cups
beans, Italian, fresh	1 to 1½ cups

beets, fresh or canned, low-sodium	¾ cup, once weekly
broccoli, fresh or frozen	1 to 1½ cups
Brussels sprouts, fresh or frozen	1 to 1½ cups
cabbage, red or white	1½ to 2 cups
carrots, fresh, frozen, or canned, no-sodium	1 to 1½ cups, once weekly
cauliflower	
fresh	¼ large head
frozen	1½ to 2 cups
collard greens, fresh or frozen	1 cup
corn, canned or frozen niblets, no-sodium	¾ cup
corn on the cob, fresh or frozen	1 5-inch ear
cucumbers, fresh, peeled	2 whole
eggplant, fresh, peeled	1½ to 2 cups
endive, fresh	2 to 3 cups
kale, fresh or frozen	1½ to 2 cups, once weekly
leeks, fresh	4 oz.
lettuce, fresh	½ average head
mushrooms, fresh	1 to 1½ cups
mustard greens, fresh or frozen	8 oz.
okra, fresh or frozen	8 oz.
onions (any kind), fresh	2 medium
peas, green, fresh, frozen, or canned, no-sodium	⅔ cup
peas, snow, fresh or frozen	4 to 6 oz.
peppers, green or red, fresh	2 whole
potato (any kind), fresh, peeled	1 medium
potato, sweet, or yam	½ average

pumpkin, fresh or canned, no-sodium	1 cup
radish, fresh	1½ to 2 cups
sprouts (any kind), fresh	1½ to 2 cups
squash, summer (includes yellow squash, zucchini, and other soft-skin squashes), fresh	1½ to 2 cups
squash, winter (includes butternut, acorn, and Hubbard squashes), fresh	⅔ cup
tomatoes fresh	2 average
canned, no-sodium	2, plus 2 tbs. juice
tomatoes, cherry, fresh	16
tomato paste, no-sodium	¼ cup
tomato sauce or puree, no-sodium	⅔ cup
turnip greens, fresh	1½ to 2 cups
turnips, white, fresh	½ cup, once weekly
turnips, yellow (rutabagas), fresh	¾ cup
water chestnuts	8 oz.

Condiments

Good news!

If you don't have any cholesterol problems, you may now add plain white vinegar to your list of permissible condiments, along with fresh lemon juice and sodium-free sweetener.

This is a "free" item and should not be counted in your seven-items-a-day quota.

You will also find a recipe for Rice House Salad Dressing in this section. Though it contains both rice and vegetables, it is also considered a "free" item. It may be used in moderation at lunch and at dinner, over rice, baked potatoes, or salads.

You may also start using small quantities of mineral oil in your cooking. Mineral oil has no calories and goes right through your body without being absorbed.

Typical Menu Plans

Breakfasts remain the same (one fruit plus one optional noncaloric beverage), but lunches and dinners may now be formulated from any combination of fruits, vegetables, and rice equivalents that appeal to you. You should still limit yourself to seven items per day, but you are no longer required to have fruit or some form of rice at meals.

Average daily menus might look something like this:

——————————————— DAY 1 ———————————————

Breakfast   ½ grapefruit
                 Decaffeinated coffee

Lunch   Vegetable soup
                 1 ear of corn on the cob
                 1 slice watermelon
                 Noncaloric beverage

Dinner   1 green pepper stuffed with tomato-rice mix
                    (counts as two items)
                 Applesauce
                 Noncaloric beverage

——————————————— DAY 2 ———————————————

Breakfast   4 stewed prunes
                 Noncaloric beverage

Lunch   Spanish rice
                   Butternut squash
                   Pineapple chunks
                   Noncaloric beverage

Dinner   Baked potato
                   Mixed salad with vinegar or lemon juice
                   Banana
                   Noncaloric beverage

--------------------- DAY 3 ---------------------

Breakfast   1 orange
                   Noncaloric beverage

Lunch   Bowl of rice covered with
                   Green pepper/mushroom/onion mix
                   Baked apple
                   Noncaloric beverage

Dinner   Baked onions in tomato sauce
                   Asparagus tips
                   Fresh fruit salad
                   Noncaloric beverage

Again, the above menus are simply examples; they are not required eating. You should feel free to select whichever permissible items you prefer. You can vary your choices, or you can stick with your favorites meal after meal (with the exception of those vegetables marked "once weekly"). *Pick foods that you enjoy.*

Recipes

Most Rice Diet recipes call for the simplest of preparations. You can't get much easier than "Peel, slice, boil, serve"!

This doesn't mean that creativity is not permitted. By all

means use whatever foods you're allowed to create combinations that will please. Below are just some of the possibilities. Each recipe makes one serving unless otherwise specified.

POTATO-RICE CAKES

Peel 1 medium-sized potato and boil until soft. Add 2 tbs. chopped onion and 2 tbs. cooked rice and mash together. Form into patties and place on pan that has been lightly greased with mineral oil. Cook in 450° oven until brown on the bottom, then turn over and bake until other side is brown.

BAKED WINTER SQUASH WITH PINEAPPLE

Cut a butternut or acorn squash in half and remove seeds. Fill cavity with pineapple chunks or crushed pineapple in its own juice. Place in pan, cover, and bake in 450° oven until squash can be easily pierced with a fork—approximately 1 hour.

BAKED YELLOW SQUASH

Slice 1 yellow squash into boiling water along with ¼ small onion, diced, and cook until both are soft. Drain and add ½ cup cooked white rice. Mash together with potato masher. Spread thinly in pan that has been lightly greased with mineral oil. Bake until brown in 450° oven. A packet of sodium-free sweetener may be added before baking, if desired.

EGGPLANT IN TOMATO SAUCE

Peel and cube eggplant and mix together with chopped onion and green pepper to taste. Add about 1 cup of Rice Diet Tomato Sauce (see Phase II, page 76, for recipe) and a packet of sodium-free sweetener (optional). Spread in a rectangular pan, cover, and bake in 450° oven until tender. One cup equals one serving.

———— BAKED ONIONS WITH TOMATOES ————

Cover a rectangular baking sheet with foil and spray with a nonstick vegetable spray. Thinly slice 2 small onions and place in a layer on top of the foil. Cover with ½ cup Rice Diet Tomato Sauce (see Phase II, page 76, for recipe) and sprinkle with sodium-free sweetener (optional). Bake in 450° oven until as hot and crusty as you like it. Alternatively, these may be broiled.

———— TOMATO-VEGETABLE SOUP ————

Use Rice Diet Tomato Sauce (see Phase II, page 76, for recipe) as a base. Add any vegetables you have on hand, cubed or cut into small pieces. Cook over low heat until vegetables are tender. If soup is too thick, add a little water while cooking. One cup equals one serving.

———— VEGETABLE SOUPS ————

Many other vegetables can be made into soups, simply by cooking them until soft, then pureeing them in a food processor. Potatoes, broccoli, and cauliflower all lend themselves well to this treatment. Thin the puree to the desired consistency by adding a little water. One cup equals one serving.

———— POTATO CHIPS ————

Bake or boil a medium-sized potato until it can easily be pierced with a fork. Slice into a pan that has been lightly greased with mineral oil. Place under the broiler until tops are brown. Turn over and brown the other sides. Serve plain or with lemon juice.

———— STUFFED GREEN PEPPERS ————

Wash a green pepper, remove the top, and clean out seeds. Stuff with a mixture of cooked rice and Rice Diet Tomato

Sauce (see Phase II, page 76, for recipe). Place in pan, cover with another ¼ cup tomato sauce, and bake, covered, in 350° oven until pepper is soft. Each whole stuffed pepper counts as two items.

RICE DIET SALAD DRESSING

Puree the following in a blender or food processor: 1 ripe peeled tomato, 1 small diced onion, the juice of 1 lemon, ½ cup cooked white rice, 1 packet of sodium-free sweetener, and ¼ cup mineral oil. Good on salads or over baked potatoes. If used within reason, this is a free item.

RUTABAGAS WITH APPLES

Peel and cube rutabaga. Boil until soft. Add a sliced apple and boil for another 3 minutes. Drain and mash together. Makes two servings.

SPANISH RICE

Add 1 cup Rice Diet Tomato Sauce (see recipe on page 76 in Phase II) to 1 cup cooked white rice. Cook over medium heat until most of the liquid evaporates and the mixture is thickened. Fresh mushrooms may be added, if you wish. Makes two servings.

CARROTS À L'ORANGE WITH RAISINS

Cook 2 carrots in ½ cup orange juice until liquid boils down and thickens around the carrots. Toss in 1 tbs. raisins and stir.

CHINESE-STYLE RICE

Spray a large frypan with nonstick vegetable spray. Cube 1 onion and 1 green pepper into pan and fry over low heat until medium soft. Add 1 to 2 cups sliced fresh mushrooms and continue cooking until all vegetables are soft. Serve over cooked rice. Fresh bean sprouts may be added, if desired. Makes two servings.

——— CABBAGE WITH APPLES AND RAISINS ———

Cook ⅛ head of cabbage with ¼ apple, cut in cubes. Boil in water to cover and drain when soft. Add 1 tbs. raisins and stir.

Miscellaneous Tips

- Because it's so important, I'll remind you again to select only the foods that you really enjoy. Don't pick cucumbers over a baked potato just to save a few calories. It's more important to plan meals that will keep you happy, and willing to stay on the diet.
- Brightly colored fruits and vegetables usually contain more vitamins than their paler cousins. Treat yourself to the best.
- If you're using lemon juice to flavor your foods, squeeze the juice over the food, rather than sucking directly on the lemon. Dr. Kempner cautions that lemon juice, applied directly to the teeth, can cause damage to the enamel.
- With the addition of fiber-rich vegetables to the diet, you should have no further need for bran. If you still choose to use it, be sure to drink an ample quantity of fluid along with it so that the bran can most efficiently do its work.
- It is better to have smaller portions of three different items at a meal than to have a triple-sized portion of just one item. Three items look and feel more like a complete meal. Moreover, excessively large portions contribute to your "food greed," and to your self-concept as an out-of-control person. A huge pile of food on a plate, even low-calorie food, is an overweight person's way of eating. Smaller portions of several items help to develop the habit of moderation.

- You've probably been hearing about some of the many salt-free sauces and condiments available at some supermarkets and specialty stores, and you're tempted. Oh, I know there are very few calories in these items, and precious little, if any, sodium. But the point is that you are trying to make adjustments that will help you over a lifetime, and changing your acquired taste for sweet or spicy foods is a good step in the right direction. You will have far greater long-term gains if you get used to the taste of unsalted, unspiced, plain and natural food.

  The trick is not to try to make plain food taste the way you love it, but to work at learning to love plain food just the way it is. That way, you can eat the foods you love and still be thin! It may take a while until you learn to appreciate the taste of plain vegetables, but with time, it *will* come to pass, and you will find yourself thoroughly enjoying each bite.

  After all, food was not meant by nature to be doctored up, its flavors hidden with spices and salt. When the lion moves in for the kill, the lioness does not come rushing up with the salt shaker. Indeed, man is the only species that adds unnatural flavoring to its food. And man is the only species suffering from an epidemic of obesity and other food-related diseases.

- Don't make a large quantity of a food, figuring that it'll last you for a while. It *will* last, but unless it's a big favorite of yours, you'll get tired of it and soon start feeling deprived.

- Never use baking soda to brighten the color of your vegetables. Baking soda contains large amounts of sodium and is therefore not permitted. Instead, run cold water over your vegetables after steaming them. This has the same brightening effect, without the unacceptable additives.

- Feel free to include potatoes at every meal if you like. Potatoes are nutritious and relatively low in calories. They've just been the victim of a bad press for many years. I promise that you can eat them daily and still quickly lose weight.

IMPORTANT NOTE: I want to say a few words about portion size and reasonableness. Although portion sizes are given for each item on the list, these quantities should be considered as guidelines, not as rules written in stone.

At the Rice House, two people at the same table can order the same item and one will, quite at random, receive substantially more than the other. Portions are not measured exactly but are, rather, dished out within an acceptable range. One of the things this diet attempts to alter is your obsessiveness about food. Being obsessive about having *exactly* two-thirds of a cup of squash is not really much better than behaving as obsessively about eating as you did before dieting.

The dangerous thing about obsessiveness is that it often leads to binging. I'm sure you're all familiar with the kind of thinking that goes, "Well, I had an extra piece of tomato, so since I've *already* broken my diet, I might as well keep on eating today and start again tomorrow." It is not uncommon for people who have overeaten even minimally to use that as justification for a full-scale binge.

To discourage such all-or-nothing thinking, this diet allows you a certain amount of leeway in measurement. Permitting a *range* in quantity encourages the development of common sense, reasonableness, and maturity about food.

Let's face it. Most people—even those with the poorest eating habits—have a pretty good idea of what a "normal" portion of food is. If you don't already know, I suggest you *learn* to judge an acceptable amount of food, then eat within that range. By all means, allow yourself a little bit more if you're particularly hungry one day. Or eat a little less on a day when you don't have that much of an appetite. And please—don't worry about the calories. A half cup of vegetables, more or less, is not going to make any real difference in your weight. Developing the ability to be *reasonable* will.

I knew one woman who claimed to have no idea at all of what constituted a "normal" portion. She would make herself a batch of fudge, pour it into an 8" × 12" pan to set, overturn the pan, then eat the fudge in one huge slab, without cutting it into pieces. The next day, she would moan, "How could I have gained weight? All I ate was *one piece* of fudge." But I can't help but think that, at heart, she really knew what she was doing all along.

It may be that you are not yet ready to handle this amount of freedom about food. If that's the case, you should stick strictly to the quantities outlined in the preceding section. If rigid rules help, then don't be a hero. Only you can be the judge of which way will work best for you to help you stay on the diet. You can always work on reasonableness later, once you've got the main part of your food problem licked.

Cheating

I promised you more "cheating" suggestions, and here they are.

If you're craving additional food and *must* have something, your best bet is to munch on cooked or raw cabbage, broccoli, cauliflower, or Brussels sprouts. All of these vegetables contain beta-carotene, which recent studies indicate has anticancer properties. If you're going to cheat, you may as well do it by feeding something healthy to your body at the same time. Carrots also contain beta-carotene, but they are too high in calories to be considered an acceptable "cheat" on this diet.

Another "cheat" that will please you is unsalted, unbuttered popcorn. Have it occasionally as a treat, if you must. Make it in the microwave, or buy yourself one of those air poppers that allow you to make it without the addition of any form of grease.

Please don't consider this as a carte blanche to eat popcorn whenever you want it. I am simply saying that if you *must* cheat (and I acknowledge that occasionally it's inevitable), there are better and worse ways of doing it.

PHASE IV: PROTEIN

"The Getting of Chicken" is a major milestone at the Rice House—the topic of many a conversation, and surely one of life's peak experiences.

Even once you "get chicken," though, you have to work your way up. First you're allowed to have it only one time a week. Then three times, then five—until, gradually, you're allowed to have it once a day, every day. Those dieting at home should follow this same gradual procedure.

And you're *never*, under any circumstances (okay, maybe once a year, on your birthday), allowed to have animal protein more than one time a day.

I expect that you, too, will feel a happy thrill upon starting to eat chicken. After all, you still love and get excited by food. Only now you're retraining yourself to pick your foods wisely.

Phase IV brings the following welcome additions to your list of permissible foods:

Chicken

One-half of a double breast (meaning one side of the breast) of a standard, 3- to 4-pound chicken. Breast only; no dark meat allowed. One half-breast supplies approximately 2 to 3 ounces of chicken. Chicken should never be fried, but may be baked, broiled, boiled, or steamed. All skin and excess fat must be removed *before* cooking.

Fish

Two to 4 ounces of any nonfatty fish. Do not eat salmon, tuna, mackerel, sardines, mullet, bluefish, herring, or pompano. All other fishes are acceptable. Select only fresh or frozen (no salt added) fish, never canned. Rinse well before cooking.

No shellfish is allowed, as it has a very high sodium

content. That means no lobster, shrimp, scampi, scallops, clams, crabmeat, oysters, mussels, etc.

Turkey

Two to 3 ounces, white meat only. Turkey may be baked, broiled, steamed, or boiled. Be sure to remove all skin and visible fat before cooking.

Although only chicken and fish are obtainable at the Rice House, it is understood that those who are vegetarians will want some other form of protein at this point.

You may therefore include the following on your list of additions in Phase IV:

Dried Peas: Includes such varieties as black-eyed, crowder, pigeon, green, and yellow. One-half cup, dry measure, before soaking and cooking.

Dried Beans: Includes garbanzos, navy, lima, kidney, red, black, brown, soy, pinto. One-half cup, dry measure, before soaking and cooking.

Legumes: Lentils, any kind, any color. One-half cup, dry measure, before soaking and cooking.

Tofu: 4 to 6 ounces, before cooking.

Recipes

Each recipe makes one serving.

———————— BAKED CHICKEN BREAST ————————

You couldn't ask for an easier recipe. Remove skin from chicken, place chicken in a pan, and cook for 20 to 30 minutes in 350° oven.

---------------------- SPANISH CHICKEN ----------------------

Remove skin from breast and place chicken in a pan. Cover with ½ cup Rice Diet Tomato Sauce (see recipe on page 76 in Phase II). Bake for 20 to 30 minutes in 350° oven. Counts as one item.

---------------------- "BREADED" FISH FILLETS ----------------------

Rub a little mineral oil on fish fillets, then dip in dry cream of rice. Lay flat on a pan lightly greased with mineral oil and bake at 450° until brown. Turn and brown on other side. Serve with lemon wedges.

These are the only recipes using animal protein to be found at the Rice House, where simplicity is the rule of the day. However, given the extensive list of fruits and vegetables that you are now allowed, you should not find it difficult to come up with many other interesting preparations. Many of your traditional favorites can be adapted to Rice Diet specifications, just by deleting all nonpermissible ingredients.

How to Cook Dried Peas, Beans, and Legumes

Wash peas, beans, or legumes thoroughly and remove any that are discolored. Soak them overnight, using 3 cups of water for every cup of dried peas or beans. Do not drain.

When you're ready to cook, bring the water to a boil, then reduce the heat and simmer the peas or beans until they are tender. Lentils and peas will require about 20 to 30 minutes to cook. Beans can take as long as 1 hour to 1½ hours.

One cup of dry peas, beans, or lentils will produce approximately 2 to 2½ cups when cooked.

Planning Your Meals

If you wish, you may now start constructing your meals somewhat differently.

Be sure to continue limiting yourself to only seven items a day, but you may now distribute your seven food items as you see fit—albeit always within the structure of your regular meals. You can choose to skip breakfast, then have three items at lunch and four at supper, or vice versa. Similarly, you may prefer a heftier breakfast (say, three items), a light lunch (one item), and a regular supper (the remaining three items).

Please note that all food items must still be eaten at mealtimes only, never as snacks.

How you choose to distribute your seven items should be decided according to what will make you *happy.*

In my case, since I don't care for breakfast, I usually chose to have three items at lunch and four at supper. I always reserved my chicken for my evening meal, so that I'd have something to look forward to all day. Moreover, I found that eating chicken at night helped me to get through the evening hours, which are always the hardest for me— and for most dieters.

Typical Menu Plans

The following plans demonstrate three different food distribution systems.

———————————— DAY 1 ————————————

(broken down into 1/3/3 items at meals)

Breakfast   ½ cantaloupe
                   Noncaloric beverage

Lunch   Zucchini in tomato sauce
                Baked potato
                Fresh peach
                Noncaloric beverage

Dinner   Baked chicken breast
                Corn on the cob
                Blueberries
                Noncaloric beverage

———————————————— DAY 2 ————————————————

(broken down into 0/3/4 items at meals)

Breakfast   Noncaloric beverage only

Lunch   Spanish rice
                Green beans
                Fresh fruit salad
                Noncaloric beverage

Dinner   Raw vegetable salad with Rice House Salad
                    Dressing
                Spanish Chicken
                Potato "chips"
                Watermelon wedge
                Noncaloric beverage

———————————————— DAY 3 ————————————————

(broken down into 2/2/3 items at meals)

Breakfast   4 prunes in prune juice
                Orange
                Noncaloric beverage

Lunch   Mixed vegetable soup
                   Banana
                   Noncaloric beverage

Dinner   "Breaded" fish fillets
                   Potato-rice cakes
                   Broccoli
                   Noncaloric beverage

Again, these are only possibilities. You should choose whatever combination of permissible foods you prefer. Remember that it's important to make yourself as happy as possible, so select foods that you really like.

Miscellaneous Tips

- Because you probably enjoy animal protein a great deal, you may be tempted to divide your daily allotment into two smaller portions, eating one portion at lunch, one at dinner. My advice is don't do this. Learn to survive, and even appreciate, a protein-free meal. You are better off working to de-emphasize the role of animal protein in your life.

- When I started skipping breakfast, I found that it helped to move my lunchtime forward a bit. Knowing that I could eat at 11:15 made it much easier for me to do without food first thing in the morning. After all, I didn't have that much longer to wait!

- At meals, eat first whatever tempts you most. There is no reason for you to have your protein and vegetables first, then your fruit as "dessert." I personally like to start my meals with a fruit. It is readily accessible and sweet, and it give me instant pleasure and gratification. It also contributes some feeling of fullness, which helps make me more satisfied with the remainder of my meal.

- You may find that you occasionally feel cold. Just put on an extra pair of socks and wait for the feeling to pass.

It's a harmless and good sign that you're well on your way to the weight loss you want.

- A woman sat down beside me at the Rice House one day and deposited on the table her bagful of spices. When someone commented, she growled, "When the doctors can prove to me why I can't have these spices, then I'll stop adding them." I didn't say anything, of course, but I'm sure you know what I thought! I find it amazing that people will give up their homes, jobs, and families, pay a substantial amount of money for medical advice, then ignore it.

  Face it—if you've got a weight problem, you *don't* have all the answers. *Do as you're told,* and keep away from those spices. Don't worry, the time is not far off when you'll be free to add many food-enhancing herbs and condiments to your diet.

- I always have my meals ready, or next to ready, so that at mealtimes, I don't have to wait very long before I eat. I know there are diet experts who advise you to select only foods that take a long time to prepare, so that you will (it is hoped) lose your appetite while you're waiting. Well, I lose my appetite, all right—but only because while I'm waiting, I'm stuffing myself with any other food I can get my hands on. When I want to eat, I want to eat, and it's counterproductive for me to have to wait a long time for the foods I'm allowed.

  I believe that for someone with an eating problem, it is preferable to have your permissible foods ready and at hand, so as not to put yourself in the position of making other, more destructive choices.

PHASE V: STARCHES, GRAINS, AND EGGS

You have now reached Phase V, what is referred to at the Rice House as "Open Diet."

It is not for everyone. Only those with no medical complications should continue to this phase. Rice Diet doctors do not permit patients with high blood pressure, diabetes, or kidney problems to go beyond Phase IV; they also require that heart size be normal and blood chemistry analyses show no real disturbance.

If you are in good health and symptom-free, and if your doctor approves, you may now make the following additions to your list of permissible foods.

Pasta

Any kind (spaghetti, macaroni, noodles, etc.), as long as it contains no salt. No spinach pasta is allowed. Salt-free pasta can be readily found in most health food stores and in many supermarkets as well.

QUANTITY: ½ cup, measured after cooking.

Bread

Any salt-free bread or rolls. Again, you are most likely to find these at your local health food store. Check labels carefully.

If you are unable to find salt-free bread in your area, you may eat regular bread, as long as salt is *last* in the list of ingredients. In this case, limit yourself to no more than 3 slices per week. And pressure your local bakeries to come out with a salt-free product you can eat *daily!*

QUANTITY: 1 slice per portion (approximately 1 ounce).

Melba Toast

Unsalted varieties only. Available in most supermarkets.

QUANTITY: 3 pieces per portion.

Matzo

Unsalted varieties only.

QUANTITY: ¾ of a piece.

Rice Cakes

Any unsalted variety. I have found these in most supermarkets, in a variety of flavors: plain, sesame, buckwheat, five-grain.

QUANTITY: 2 cakes equal one portion.

Pretzels

Any unsalted variety.

QUANTITY: ¾ of an ounce.

Tortillas

Salt-free. Available in most supermarkets.

QUANTITY: 1 tortilla.

Grains

Oatmeal or rolled oats, ⅔ of a cup, cooked.
Cornmeal, white or yellow, whole ground, ¼ cup, dry measure.

Grits, ⅔ cup, cooked.

Farina, ⅔ cup, cooked.

Bulgur, ⅔ cup, cooked.

Couscous, ⅔ cup, cooked.

Millet, ⅔ cup, cooked.

Buckwheat (kasha), ⅔ cup, cooked.

Cracked wheat, ⅔ cup, cooked.

Eggs

If your blood chemistry is in order, and if you do not have high blood pressure, kidney problems, or diabetes, you may now add a limited number of eggs to your diet. They may be boiled, poached, coddled, scrambled, or cooked sunny-side-up. For the last two, use mineral oil, a Teflon pan, or one of the nonstick, sodium-free vegetable sprays.

QUANTITY: 1 egg, any size, equals one portion. Do not eat eggs more than four times a week, and do not have more than 1 egg on any given day. On the days that you eat an egg, eat only half the portion of any other form of protein that you select.

Condiments

As promised in the Phase IV section, there's good news on the condiment front. The following items may now be included and are "free." They should not be counted as part of your seven daily items.

Vinegar: If you have no cholesterol problem, you may now have any type of vinegar, as long as there is no salt or sodium in the list of ingredients. Start experimenting with red wine vinegar, cider vinegar, etc., on your salads and in your recipes.

Garlic and Onion: Fresh only, for flavoring purposes. No garlic powder or onion powder. And you *know* you're not allowed any garlic salt or onion salt!

Dill: Fresh only, not dried.

Parsley: Any kind, fresh only.

Honey: Maximum 1 tablespoon per day.

Mustard: Dry, powdered mustard only. No prepared mustards.

Vegetable Sprays: Regular or butter-flavored. Read labels carefully to be sure the sprays contain no sodium.

Typical Menu Plans

You're now allowed so many different foods that you should find it easy to come up with a variety of delicious dishes. The following are some menus for representative days. As before, they illustrate possibilities, and are not required eating.

——————————— DAY 1 ———————————

Breakfast   1 rice cake (equals half a portion)
1 slice of melon
Noncaloric beverage

Lunch   Omelet with dill
½ slice toast (equals half a portion)
Strawberries
Noncaloric beverage

Dinner   Turkey
Cranberry dressing
Apple-raisin stuffing
Noncaloric beverage

——————————— DAY 2 ———————————

Breakfast   Poached egg on
1 slice toast
Noncaloric beverage

Lunch   Baked potato with carrot-parsley puree
Fruit cobbler
Noncaloric beverage

Dinner   Minestrone with pasta and beans
Fresh peach
Noncaloric beverage

———————————— DAY 3 ————————————

Breakfast   Oatmeal with honey
                 Noncaloric beverage

Lunch   Raw vegetable plate with cider vinegar
                 dressing
                 Spaghetti with tomato sauce
                 Noncaloric beverage

Dinner   Chicken Melba
                 Spanish rice
                 Strawberry-rhubarb compote
                 Noncaloric beverage

Recipes

Each recipe makes one serving unless otherwise specified.

———————————— HERBED OMELET ————————————

Whip up 1 egg with 1 tbs. water and 1 tsp. fresh chopped parsley or dill. Fry over low heat in a pan sprayed with nonstick vegetable spray. When dry on the bottom, flip and cook on the other side.

———————————— EGG ON A MOUND ————————————

Boil cauliflower and broccoli together until tender. Remove from heat, drain, and puree in a food processor or blender. Make a mound on a plate and, with the back of a spoon, make a slight indentation. Poach 1 egg in boiling water, remove with slotted spoon, and place on top of mound. (Alternately, the egg can be cooked sunny-side-up with nonstick vegetable spray.) Sprinkle with chopped parsley or dill. Counts as two items.

FRENCH TOAST

Whip 1 egg with a fork and soak a slice of bread in it until the bread has completely absorbed the egg. Broil the bread on both sides until brown. Can be served plain or sprinkled with sodium-free sweetener or with "free" honey.

— BREAD PUDDING WITH LEMON HONEY SAUCE —

Whip up 1 egg with 1 tbs. water and 1 packet of sodium-free sweetener. Remove crust from 1 slice bread and then tear bread into small pieces. Stir into egg and keep mixing until all egg has been absorbed. Add 1 tbs. raisins. Grease a small baking dish with mineral oil, pile in mixture, and bake at 350° until top is brown and pudding is set, about 15 minutes.

For the sauce, add fresh lemon juice to your "free" honey portion until you get just the mixture of sweet and tart that you like. Pour sauce over pudding and serve warm or cold. Makes two servings.

APPLE-RAISIN STUFFING

Mix 1 slice bread with 1 tbs. raisins, ½ apple, diced or grated, and ¼ cup water. Stir and bake at 350° until brown.

POTATO-GREEN PEPPER OMELET

Slice 1 medium-sized potato thinly and lay flat on a baking sheet that has been lightly greased with mineral oil. Slice ½ green pepper into strips and add to pan. Squeeze lemon juice over all and broil until brown, stirring from time to time. Whip up 1 egg with 1 tbs. water and drizzle over vegetables. Makes two servings or counts as two items.

CHICKEN EGG DROP SOUP

Boil 1 chicken breast in 1 cup water until chicken separates easily from bone. Remove chicken to serve at another time and skim fat off remaining liquid. Whip up an egg and slowly pour it into the boiling chicken stock, stirring with a fork all the while. The egg will cook in long, thin strips. Add 1 tbs. chopped parsley and 1 tsp. lemon juice, if desired. Serve hot. Counts as one item.

CHICKEN MELBA

Crush allotted portion of melba toast and mix with fresh chopped parsley or dill. Moisten chicken in water and roll thoroughly in crumbs. Bake uncovered in 350° oven for 20 to 30 minutes. Counts as two items.

EGG IN A BASKET

Boil fresh asparagus tips until soft. Toast 1 slice bread and arrange asparagus over toast. Top with a poached egg and sprinkle with chopped parsley.

SPICY CROUTONS

Grate fresh onion and/or garlic buds. Stir in 1 slice bread, cut into small cubes. Spread in a baking pan that has been lightly greased with mineral oil. Broil, stirring occasionally, until brown and crispy on all sides.

CHICKEN DIABLO

Put "free" portion of honey in a small dish and stir in dry mustard to taste. Remove skin from chicken breast and coat chicken on all sides with honey-mustard mixture. Place in pan and bake, uncovered, in 350° oven for 20 to 30 minutes.

A Discussion About Calories

As you know by now, this is not a diet on which you have to count calories. If you follow the guidelines, your daily caloric intake will automatically stay within an acceptable range. However, you may have noticed that most of the portions of food you're allowed contain approximately 100 calories each. This means that you are taking in an average of 700 calories a day.

This is a relatively small amount of food, and it may well be that there are some days when it just doesn't meet your needs. Whether it's for physical or emotional reasons, there will be times you want more.

The answer is easy. Allow yourself an additional "item" of food. Or even more, if necessary. There are some occasions when you simply feel hungrier, and you know that you're going to eat. At these times, it is far better to increase the number of acceptable items you eat than to go foraging outside your list of permissible foods.

You really cannot do yourself much damage by adding an extra fruit or another baked potato. Even the occasional extra portion of chicken or bread won't really hurt. And you'll feel a lot better, both physically and psychologically, about what you're putting in your mouth. So if you're "needing" extra food, make selections from any of the five phases, and don't worry, even if on occasion your caloric intake goes up to 1000 calories or more. There will be days when you're not particularly hungry (it happens!), and if you're wise, you'll use those days to eat *less* than your allotted seven items, to compensate.

I'm not saying that calories don't count, just that you shouldn't count them. Strive to limit yourself to your allotted seven items, but realize that in the normal order of things, your daily intake will vary between 500 and 1000 calories, and that's perfectly all right.

Face it. There are some days when it's useless trying to impose a severe calorie limit on yourself. You are not two people, one "policing" the other. Accept that there are times when you need to be gentle with yourself—and that might occasionally mean eating a reasonable quantity of extra food.

Miscellaneous Tips

- "Open Diet" means that, if you so wish, you can eat any or all of the foods included in phases I through V. However, you do not *have* to select any of the new additions. You are always free to eat meals from any previous phase. For example, you may not wish to have an entire day of rice and fruit, but you very well may enjoy eating them occasionally for lunch, followed by your regular Phase V dinner at night.

  How do you decide? Basically, choose what you *want*—whatever appeals to you and will give you pleasure. Ask yourself before meals, "What do I *feel* like eating right now?"

- People often ask me if you lose more weight on fruit and rice than you do once you're on the other phases. Although the calorie count is the same if you choose to eat vegetables and protein, plain rice and fruit *do* seem to take weight off the most quickly—another reason for including the occasional fruit and rice meal in your menu. Moreover, for those of you nearing your goal weight, you will find that rice and fruit often accelerate the loss of those difficult last few pounds.

- I believe that you should banish all dangerous (non-permissible but tempting) foods from your home. There are now so many foods on your permissible list that all members of your household should be able to find something that pleases them. To those who say it is "not fair" to other family members to have to do without, I would counter that it is "not fair" to make your very difficult diet battle even harder.

  The consequences of your eating the wrong foods are far greater than any consequences *others* "suffer" by doing without. In my opinion, it is more unreasonable for nondieters (especially those who say they love you) to expect you to resist the foods you can't have than it is for you to ask them to forego them for a while. Indeed, given the quality of most of the snack foods on the market, you are probably doing them a favor!

- Here we are in Phase V, "Open Diet," and still no sign of dairy products. That's right. The time-honored theory that milk is the ideal food for everyone has been disputed by the Rice Diet. In fact, Dr. Kempner contends that a quart of milk can be more deadly to some than a quart of rotgut whisky! Dairy products contain a good deal of sodium and are also quite high in saturated fat and calories. You'll have to wait until you reach goal weight before adding them to your diet.

- I have always had very definite opinions about what is the "best part" of most foods. It astonished me no end when I discovered that most thin people don't even understand the concept of "best part." But I'm sure *you* know exactly what I mean! Depending on the particular food, the "best part" is the inside or the outside, the bottom or the top, the crunchy part or the soft. We all have our preferences.

My suggestion is that you eat the part you like best *first,* rather than saving it for last, as most food lovers do. The reason for this suggestion is that if you save the best part for last, you're going to eat the entire thing *for sure,* just to get to your favorite part. You certainly aren't going to leave it, if I know you! You'll just keep on eating, right down to the end, even if you're no longer very hungry.

If, on the other hand, you eat your favorite part first, there's an outside chance that you may decide to forego some of the "inferior" remainder, and eat less. Moreover, it makes sense to eat the part you prefer at the beginning, while you're at your hungriest. That way, you'll enjoy it more. If you first dull your appetite with less-favored parts, you're depriving yourself of the full pleasure you could have obtained from your food.

- Honey or sweetener? The answer to this question comes down to a choice between chemicals and calories. Honey has 60 calories per tablespoon, while sweetener is calorie-free and does the same job. My choice was to use sweetener while I was concentrating on losing weight, then I switched to honey once the main part of the job was done.

CHAPTER NINE

Phase VI: Maintenance Recommendations

STICKING TO the Rice Diet and achieving Dr. Kempner's goal weight makes a very definite statement about you. It shows you to be someone who can DO IT—someone who is able to consider alternatives, choose wisely, and do what is best for yourself.

If you are capable of such discipline and effort, you don't need to be told exactly, to the quarter cup, what you should eat at each meal. You don't need precise measurements or directions—you need only call upon the personal power and strength of character that you have already demonstrated.

For this reason, a maintenance "diet" should not be an excessively detailed regimen, but rather, a mature commitment to proper eating that you make because you are truly ready and willing to make this choice and abide by it. A rigid diet is a suitable approach for those who have not yet developed constructive eating habits. Maintenance, on the other hand, assumes that the dieter has learned something during the process of losing weight.

In a sense, "Maintenance" is just another word for maturity. It supposes a mature awareness of the facts of life (you cannot eat whatever you want and still be thin) and the willingness to make mature choices based on this reality.

You've demonstrated your maturity by going all the way to goal. Why should you now start treating yourself like a child?

Thus maintenance, Rice Diet-style, offers you not a rigid diet but a set of intelligent guidelines to live by. If you choose to live by them, you will never again have problems with your weight.

Maintenance comes down to a commitment to the following resolutions—on the whole. By ''on the whole,'' I mean that although you will not always do all of these things, in general you will undertake to live your life according to these principles.

1. I will limit my eating to two or three meals a day. (Many find they prefer to skip one of their daily meals, but this is certainly not necessary, and you should feel free to have all three.)
2. I will not try to eat as much food as possible at meals. Rather, I will try to eat as little as possible, always consistent with meeting my physical needs.
3. I will eat my meals at regular times, generally within a two-hour range. For example, lunch will be between 11 A.M. and 1 P.M., dinner between 6 and 8 P.M. Naturally, you will pick whatever two-hour span best suits your needs.
4. I will eat predominantly Rice Diet foods: fruits, grains, vegetables, and optionally a small amount of animal protein.
5. I will avoid eating between meals. When I do snack between meals, I will try to limit myself to Rice Diet foods. Let's face it—''binging'' on fruits, grains, and vegetables represents a giant step forward in control!
6. I will only infrequently eat those foods that I know are bad for me, not only because they cause me to gain weight, but also because they arouse cravings that I prefer to avoid. I don't want to get caught up in that food misery again!
7. On those occasions when I do partake of harmful foods, I will try to eat only my very favorites. That way, I will at least maximize the pleasure of the experience.

8. I will return to the Rice Diet (any phase, it doesn't matter) as soon as I've put on more than one or two pounds. I want to catch the problem early, as it can so easily get out of hand. A few bad days may not make that much of a difference on the scale, but the longer I let it go, the harder it will be to get back on the diet.

The wise (and mature!) dieter will recognize that going from a diet to maintenance should not be equated with serving time, then being released from jail. You've obtained wonderful results with this pure and healthy program. Why stop doing what so obviously works? As the old saying goes, "If it isn't broken, don't fix it." You've found a diet that works—hang on to it, don't let it go!

The Maintenance Phase of the Rice Diet is an extension and liberalization of the original plan. It is not a rigid formula but a synthesis of everything we know to date about proper nutrition. It can be one thing today and slightly modified tomorrow, as new information about nutrition filters in. Happily, nutrition is at last getting the attention it deserves, and a good deal of helpful research is being done in this field.

You will be happy to learn that what we have been re-ferring to as "Rice Diet allowables" will now include a great many more foods. To put it in one sentence, the rule of thumb is:

WHATEVER NATURE PUT ON EARTH FOR MAN TO EN-JOY IS ACCEPTABLE TO EAT—AS LONG AS WISDOM, MODERATION, AND INTELLIGENCE ARE EMPLOYED.

This means that virtually all natural foods may now be included in your diet, as long as certain restrictions and limitations are observed. For example, common sense will tell you that though it's hard to OD on radishes, an excess of peanuts—equally natural!—will do you in.

Note: It is important that you continue to be checked by your physician. Any changes in your diet should be discussed fully before additions or alterations are made. Your lifelong eating plan should be tailor-made for you.

MAKING THE TRANSITION

How you move from dieting to maintenance requires considerable planning and work. Essentially, you will be devising a lifetime, individualized eating plan for yourself. Like the rest of the Rice Diet, this involves a well-thought-out, gradual, step-by-step process.

There are three main variables that must be considered.

How Much Can I Eat and Still Maintain My Loss?

Like you, I have seen many formulas for calculating how many calories one can eat and still maintain a given weight. These usually involve multiplying your ideal weight by some arbitrary figure, which varies according to how active you are.

I am wary of these formulas. First, to find two that agree with each other is quite a feat. Second, I do not believe that the whole world can be neatly divided into three categories: sedentary, moderately active, and very active.

To my mind, it is only by actually testing foods on your body that you will discover how much you personally can eat and still maintain your weight.

At this point, the Rice Diet becomes a question of calories. Until now, you've been eating approximately 700 calories a day. Now, at Maintenance, you'll be starting to slowly increase this amount.

To do this, you will need a first-class calorie book, one that lists almost any food you can think of. You'd also be wise to pick up one of those pocket-sized versions, to carry with you when away from home. Armed with this data, you're now ready to start considering additions to your diet.

I recommend that each week you add no more than 100 to 200 calories to your daily intake, always selecting from Rice Diet foods *only* at this point.

In other words, once you have reached goal, increase your calorie intake to 800 or 900 calories a day, then stay there for one full week to see how you do. Assuming that you don't gain, add another 100 calories a day, and spend the next week at 1000 calories. The next week, move to 1100 calories, etc.

Keep a strict eye on the scale, in order to observe the effects. When you reach the point of leveling off (when you find the number of calories at which you neither lose nor gain), you have identified the maximum number of calories you can eat on a daily basis.

After you know this figure you are ready for the next step, which involves incorporating new foods into your dietary plan.

IMPORTANT NOTE: ALL ADDITIONS MUST BE MADE *AT MEALS ONLY*, NEVER IN THE FORM OF SNACKS.

How Do I Add Foods to My Diet?

The addition of new foods requires experimentation, patience, and time. Basically, you will be proceeding along the same continuum begun in Phase I, gradually adding an assortment of additional foods to your meals. (The Basic Maintenance Plan that follows, beginning on page 114, will provide details about which foods are now allowed.)

Please proceed with great caution. You may now be thin, but that doesn't mean you're cured. For safety's sake, it is important to build your maintenance program around your own particular weaknesses and strengths.

I recommend that new foods be added only one at a time. Don't rush off to the supermarket and stock up on the new group of allowables.

Consider the process to be a little like testing for allergies. If you find that a particular food causes you to overindulge, leave it out. If you wish, you can try it again in a few months to see if you've learned to handle it better over time. You *do* become wiser about food as you continue to eat right.

I also recommend that you add your favorite foods last. First add the items that you find easiest to handle. You're still much too fragile to expose yourself to unnecessary temptation.

When Will I Be Allowed to Include Snacks in My Diet?

Because this one can be treacherous, it is the last variable to consider. You shouldn't even consider eating at any time other than meals until you have the first two variables well under control.

I am against snacking (which doesn't mean that I never do it!), but if it's important to you, you must structure your eating so that some calories are put aside for snacks.

Don't snack indiscriminately, whenever the mood strikes you. Again, it's wiser to accustom your body to a specific routine. If you know that you like a late-night snack, schedule it within a certain time period each night. The same goes for mid-morning or mid-afternoon breaks.

Snacks should be limited to fresh fruits and vegetables. High-protein items should be eaten exclusively at meals. Be sure to deduct the snack calories you've used from your permissible daily total.

And *do* consider giving up snacking completely. After all, what do you really need it for? Focusing on eating two or three times a day is sufficient. Snacking simply extends your preoccupation with food.

THE BASIC MAINTENANCE PLAN

The following categories of foods may now be added to your daily food plan, assuming that your doctor agrees that they're okay for you to eat. Please take my comments and reservations into consideration when devising your own personal maintenance plan.

Dairy Products

Dairy products contain calcium and protein, and for those without health or weight problems, they can be excellent and nutritious foods. Unfortunately, they also contain large quantities of saturated fats, sodium, cholesterol—and calories. For example, in order to get the recommended amount of calcium in your diet, you would have to drink five 8-ounce glasses of milk each and every day. Even if you drank only skim milk, you would still be taking in close to 500 calories, which is a sizable portion of your daily calorie allowance.

You might want to consider taking calcium pills instead. Or, possibly, taking some of your calcium through dairy products and the rest in pill form. (I'd love to have my calcium in *scoop* form, if you know what I mean, but I fight the urge!)

If you choose to include dairy foods in your diet, stick exclusively to skim milk products. And please, strictly limit your intake, for these foods can cause problems, both with weight and with health. I personally eat absolutely no dairy products at all.

Milk: Half the calories in whole milk are fat, and half of *those* are saturated fat. Removing this excess fat in no way impairs the quality of the protein and calcium found in milk. If you're going to drink milk, or add it to your coffee, make sure that you select only skim milk.

Butter: Butter should be avoided, and oils should be substituted whenever fats are required. (See the section on fats, page 118.) If you insist on having butter, at least make sure that it's the unsalted kind.

Yogurt: If included in your diet, yogurt should be the plain, unsweetened, skim milk variety. Feel free to

add your own fresh fruits to it, along with a little
sodium-free sweetener, or honey, if you wish.

Cheese: I know, I know, you love it—but it's a very
high-fat, high-sodium, high-calorie food. If you're
determined to have it, look for unsalted cheeses,
available in health food stores and some cheese specialty shops. Though unsalted cheeses have no
added salt, they are far from sodium-free, since milk
naturally contains a good deal of sodium. Unsalted
cheeses are definitely an acquired taste, but appreciation *does* come with time, and if you *must* eat
cheese, they are by far the best bet.

Cheese should be eaten only at meals, never as a
snack. For each ounce of cheese that you eat, cut
out 2 ounces of any other form of protein eaten that
day. Limit yourself to a maximum of 4 ounces of
hard cheese per week.

Animal Protein

Study after study has implicated animal fat in the development of cancer, and there is no form of animal protein
completely free of animal fat. I don't know about you, but
I don't need much more convincing than that to eliminate
animal protein from my diet. And most cardiologists agree
that a diet of fruits, vegetables, and grains is the one best
suited to man's needs.

It also seems to me that if the Creator had wanted us
to be meat eaters, He would have given us fangs and
claws, as He did all other carnivores. Man is an omni-
vore, which means he is capable of eating anything—but
just because it's *possible* doesn't mean it's a good idea.

If you limit animal protein to chicken, turkey, and fish,
you may now increase the amount you eat to a maximum
of 6 ounces per day. Or you may occasionally choose to
eat the following instead.

Poultry: Gourmet fowl, like duck and goose, may now
be included, as long as you limit your portion to 2

to 3 ounces. These are very fatty birds, and all fat and skin should be removed before cooking.

Seafood: The fattier fishes, like salmon, tuna, mackerel, sardines, and bluefish, may now be included. Limit yourself to 3 to 4 ounces. Avoid smoked fish. You may also select small portions of shellfish, such as shrimp, scallops, lobster, crabmeat, oysters, etc. These foods are very high in sodium, so make sure you have no more than 2 to 3 ounces.

Beef, Lamb, Pork, Veal: These meats may now be included, as long as all visible fat is removed before cooking. Select lean cuts, and limit yourself to 2 to 3 ounces. Veal is the leanest of the bunch, and therefore your best bet. Never eat processed meats (e.g., cold cuts, hot dogs), as they contain large amounts of sodium and sodium nitrate, a suspected carcinogen. Avoid smoked or canned meats.

Organ Meats: Such foods as liver, kidneys, brains, and sweetbreads may be included in limited fashion (2 to 3 ounces). Since they are very high in cholesterol, they should be eaten a maximum of once a week.

Nuts and Seeds

Though undeniably delicious, and even nutritious, these are very high-fat, high-calorie items, and you'll have to watch carefully if you choose to include them in your diet. What makes them worse is that it's hard to stop with just a few. As the old saying goes, "Who can eat just one peanut?"

I'm nuts about nuts, and tend to overdo, so though I'll occasionally eat them, I never keep them in the house. Unless you have an iron constitution, I recommend you do the same.

All kinds of nuts and seeds are now allowed, though certainly not the salted varieties. Avoid prepared mixtures, like hiker's mix, which contains who knows what. But feel free to make your own fruit and nut combinations.

Peanut butter and other nut butters are also allowed (at meals only), as long as they are made without the addition of sugar and salt. Pure nut butters are available in any health food store, and they are every bit as delicious as the doctored-up kind. Often the store will have a nut grinder on the premises and will make the butter for you fresh.

Pure nut butters tend to separate after sitting a while—the oil contained in the nuts rises to the top. Instead of mixing it back in, why not just pour it off? That way, you'll still get the delicious taste, while cutting down on calories, at least to some extent.

Fats

Fats contain 9 calories per gram, as compared with the 4 calories per gram found in protein and carbohydrates. An excess of fats can lead to heart disease and stroke, so quantities should be strictly monitored at all times.

If your cholesterol has not been stabilized at a normal level, you should avoid fats completely, unless your physician indicates otherwise.

I occasionally use oil in salads or for cooking, but I never touch butter, margarine, or mayonnaise—all of which I used to love all too well. My tastes have changed to the point where I now find greasy food downright nauseating, and boy, am I glad that I've come to feel that way!

Butter: Butter is a natural food, but it is a saturated fat, and it's best to avoid it completely. As mentioned earlier, if you must have it, use only the unsalted variety.

Margarine: Margarine is not a pure food and for that reason alone cannot be included. What's worse, the manufacture of margarine involves hydrogenation, and hydrogenated fats have been linked to the development of cancer. Moreover, though you may not realize it, margarine contains exactly the same number of calories as butter.

Mayonnaise: Pure, salt-free mayonnaise can be found in health food stores, and if you must have it, this is the only acceptable kind. However, even salt-free mayonnaise usually contains eggs and either sugar or honey, so this is a product that is far better eliminated from your diet. Try eating sandwiches "straight," and I'll bet you hardly notice the difference.

Oils: Of all the items in this category, oils are the only form of fat I can recommend, as long as they are eaten in moderation (no more than 1 tablespoon per day). Polyunsaturated oils, such as sunflower oil or safflower oil, are your best bets, as well as such natural vegetable oils as corn oil. Mineral oil remains a freebie, and can often be substituted for other oils.

Sweets

What can I say about sweets that you don't already know? For most dieters, sweets can lead to big trouble. On the other hand, we're only human. I still occasionally indulge, but I *never* keep them in the house. Nor should you. At least make yourself go out to get them if you want them.

For sweetening foods, sugar and honey are your best bets. Molasses, corn syrup, and maple syrup contain too much sodium. Even better, stick to sodium-free artificial sweeteners, and save yourself a lot of potential grief.

Fruits

Go ahead, enjoy. Just keep an eye on exactly how much you're eating, as fruits can consume your calorie allotment fast.

The only fruit excluded up to this point is dates, and yes, you may now add them to your diet. You may also add salt-free fruit jams, jellies, and marmalades, sweetened either artificially or with sugar and honey. Naturally, the former have far fewer calories, and they can readily be found in all health food stores.

Vegetables

You may now add fatty vegetables like avocados and olives, as well as the saltier vegetables like spinach, celery, watercress, and beets. However, because of their fat and/or sodium content, your intake of these vegetables should be limited to moderate portions.

Eggs

Your limit remains the same: a maximum of 4 whole eggs per week. Deduct 2 ounces from your daily protein allotment each time you eat an egg, and never eat more than 1 egg a day.

You may, if you wish, eat additional egg *whites*. An egg white contains very few calories, and it can be delicious whipped up into an omelet, especially when flavored with such items as fresh parsley or dill. Each egg white means deducting 1 ounce from your daily protein allowance.

Spices, Herbs, and Condiments

Although these are now permitted, I personally never use any seasoning on my food other than sodium-free sweetener and lemon juice. In fact, I hardly ever use even those. With the passage of time, I have become accustomed to the taste of plain, pure food, and now I actually *prefer* to eat food that way. Again, this was a matter of developing a new habit, and it paid off wonderfully for me. Give it time, and you'll feel the same.

The following may now be added to your diet, in small quantities:

Herbs	Spices	Seeds
basil	allspice	anise
bay leaf	cinnamon	caraway
chives	cardamom	dill
cilantro	cloves	poppy
cumin	curry	sesame
fennel	mustard	
ginger	nutmeg	
garlic	paprika	
horseradish	pepper	
marjoram	saffron	
mint	turmeric	
oregano		
parsley		
rosemary		
sage		
savory		
tarragon		
thyme		

The salt-free section of your supermarket will have some prepared condiments that are now acceptable on this program.

Salt

If you are a Group A dieter, you may now start to include small amounts of salt in your diet, including such items as plain salt, onion salt, garlic salt, celery salt, and soy sauce. Limit yourself to a maximum of one-sixteenth of a teaspoon per day. Since this amount of salt is hard to measure, perhaps you'll decide to skip the whole thing instead. Good for you! Remember to keep submitting urine samples to your physician for analysis of salt content. This will help in formulating your own personal Maintenance Plan.

Those who have had a serious weight problem should never again in their lives eat salt. Dr. Kempner maintains that some of us have bodies that just aren't able to handle it. We respond with what is almost an allergic reaction. As he points out, if someone is allergic to poison ivy, just one small leaf can cause them to break out. In the same way, even a tiny bit of salt can cause serious problems for those with "the disease."

I *never* touch salt, though I occasionally eat foods that contain it when I binge. But I have become so sensitive to salt that I can taste minute quantities of it, even in a cookie. I'm happy and relieved that salt is by and large out of my life.

Alcoholic Beverages

Though not a food, this category is unquestionably of interest to many dieters. Moderate amounts of alcohol are compatible with the Maintenance Phase of the Rice Diet, as long as sodium concentrates are less than 2.0 mEq/qt. Frankly, I have no idea what that complicated equation stands for, but I know it means that the following drinks are your best bets:

White Wines: Most German and French varieties.

Red Wines: Preferably those from Germany, France, and Spain.

Rosé Wines: By and large, those from Portugal and Spain are best.

I regret that American wines are not included on this list, but their sodium content can be as much as thirty times higher than that of those wines listed above. Perhaps domestic wineries could give this problem some thought.

Liquor: Most hard liquors are low in sodium and therefore acceptable. Be careful to watch the sodium content of the mixers, however.

Beer: Most American brands are just fine. Why not stick with the Lites and cut down on calories?

As long as you watch the number of calories you're consuming, you can feel comfortable having the occasional low-sodium drink. Be careful, however, if drinking makes you relax your vigilance about food.

One Last Word

The emphasis in your Maintenance Plan should be on fruits, vegetables, and grains—or, as Dr. Kempner puts it, the foods available to man in the Garden of Eden. Include yellow-orange and leafy green vegetables daily, as well as some form of Vitamin C (citrus fruits, melons, berries, and tomatoes). Include small portions of lean animal protein if you wish.

As for the new inclusions—well, they are natural and therefore permitted. But you should bear in mind that they are, for the most part, higher in calories than the foods permitted until now. In one way or another, many of them can cause long-term ills. By all means, add them to your diet, but please use wisdom and restraint.

ADAPTATIONS

The Basic Maintenance Plan is state-of-the-art nutrition, and certainly it is the only option I would consider for myself. However, I realize that not all of you will want to eat like this for the rest of your lives, and I have therefore come up with some alternate approaches.

The next best thing to full-time Basic Maintenance is Partial Maintenance, supplemented by "regular" food. Essentially, these formulas are mixtures of Rice Diet eating with "regular" food. As a way of life, I can't endorse them, but properly monitored, they *will* keep you thin.

The Partial Maintenance Plan involves selecting one of the following options, for example:

1. For those with active social lives, eat Basic Main-

tenance at all times, except when invited out or when you entertain.

2. For those who like to eat on weekends, eat Basic Maintenance all week and ''regular'' food Saturday and Sunday.

3. Eat Rice Diet lunches (any phase) and ''regular'' food at dinner.

Or you may wish to design your own variation. Just be sure that the ratio of Rice Diet meals to ''regular'' meals keeps your weight where you want it.

I must tell you frankly that I have difficulty with these plans. I can't help but think that by eating this way you place yourself at constant risk. It's hard to go back on a diet Monday after a weekend of calorie splurging!

Still, it is entirely possible that those in Groups A and B can handle these adaptations well. I suppose that not everyone has to be a fanatic, like me!

THE BAND-AID APPROACH

This form of maintenance should be considered only by people in Group A—those Almost-Thins who have never had too big a battle with weight.

Most Group A dieters will need the Rice Diet for only a few weeks. This short space of time may not be enough to convince you of the benefits of changing your eating habits for life, especially if you've never had much of a problem with control. For those of you who want to use the diet to lose some weight but are uninterested in it as a permanent way of life, you might try the Band-Aid, or Finger-in-the-Dike, approach.

Get to goal, ascertain how many calories you can eat in a day and still keep off your weight, then limit yourself to that amount of calories while eating your ''regular'' foods.

The crucial thing, of course, will be to catch any gain before it can cause concern. My recommendation is the 10 percent rule. If you see that you've put on 10 percent of the weight you lost, go back on the Rice Diet (any phase) until the weight is off again.

MAINTENANCE TIPS

Even those accustomed to the diet are now facing a new set of circumstances. The following tips will offer some direction and help.

Preparing Meals

- Most North Americans use pepper and salt as their primary seasoning. Unless you opt to eat your food totally unseasoned, as I do, start experimenting with various spices and herbs. Just don't go overboard. Let's face it— if it's delicious, you'll want more. It is not important that your food be delicious, because if it isn't, you're more likely to be satisfied with *enough*.
- Regular baking powder and baking soda are sodium compounds and should be avoided. Low-sodium equivalents can be found in health food stores.
- Many cookbooks, especially vegetarian cookbooks, offer recipes that can easily be adapted to Rice Diet specifications. Either make acceptable substitutions for nonacceptable items (e.g., oil for butter) or delete them entirely. In most cases, you'll never notice the difference.
- Frozen apple juice concentrate can often be substituted for the sugar called for in a recipe, in equal amounts.

At the Table

- When you're maintaining, be sure to eat only foods you like. There should never be a time when you select foods you don't like. Your meals should provide you with pleasure, and not involve self-sacrifice and deprivation.

- On the other hand, if you like any particular food *a lot*, be leery of it! Foods you just love can be too hard to handle.
- Stick to moderate portions of whatever you're allowed. Not even acknowledged diet foods, such as salads, should be eaten in quantities larger than average because of the destructive feelings of gluttony this can arouse. Instead, have smaller portions of several different items.
- You most certainly do not have to eat all of the calories that you're allowed. By all means, cut back when you're not particularly hungry. Rest assured that the occasional day of overindulgence is bound to come along to balance things out.
- Your last bite of food at a meal should never be one of your favorite items. That just leaves you with a delicious and stimulating taste in your mouth—and all too often, the desire to have more. You're better off finishing up with something rather bland, instead of a temptation that might lead to excess.
- Keep working at distancing yourself from food. Consider leaving one bite of everything on your plate. Or think about undertaking an occasional one-day fast. Stretch yourself, work on building up your indifference to food.

Shopping for Food

- Experiment with unfamiliar foods on the acceptable list. Find a recipe and make small quantities. You're bound to be turned on to a few new healthy and natural foods, and this will add variety to your diet.
- Dried fruits are an excellent substitute for sweets. My favorites are packaged Calimyrna figs, which are a delight to all five senses.
- Avoid all refined and processed foods, most of which are very high in sodium. Moreover, nutrients are often

reduced during processing, as is fiber content. These are definitely not the best foods for you to eat.

- If you *must* buy prepared or canned foods, shop in the low-sodium section of your supermarket. And read all labels carefully—don't skip a word.

MISCELLANEOUS TIPS

- Keep up your exercise routine (see Chapter 10). Exercise should be considered a permanent part of your new life.
- Keep weighing yourself daily—remember the advantages of dealing with reality. You'll want to catch a weight gain immediately, before it's out of control.
- Keep seeing your doctor until and unless he or she advises you that it is no longer necessary to keep in frequent touch.
- Each morning, plan what you're going to eat during the day, and be sure that you have those foods on hand and ready. A food plan may appear to be a restriction, but in fact it's liberating, since it releases your mind from its focus on food. Moreover, mealtimes, when you're hungry, are surely the worst times to be deciding what you're going to eat.
- If you find yourself craving something that's not on your food plan, console yourself with the knowledge that you can schedule it in the next day—if you still want it.
- To some extent, maintenance requires trial and error. How do you *know* you can't keep peanut butter in the house unless you try it? You should therefore expect to make some mistakes and have some setbacks. No problem—as long as you learn from them. You are engaged in gathering the evidence that will help you construct a tailor-made Maintenance Plan for yourself.
- There are very few overweight people who walk straight and proud, with the result that posture is sometimes a problem for those who lose weight. When I

first tried to deal with this issue, I walked with my shoulders thrust back. This felt unnatural and looked pretty stiff, to boot. The trick I now use is to think of my rib cage and keep it straight. If you concentrate on keeping the section from your waist to your underarms erect, the rest of your body will fall gracefully into place. This holds true when you are standing, sitting, or in any position at all.

SUMMATION

Maintenance involves eating appropriate foods in an appropriate manner. It is the calm, willing acceptance of the fact that your eating habits must change for life.

Admittedly, for someone who loves to eat, the prospect of doing without your favorite foods can be daunting. Some people consider eliminating favorites as a fate worse than death.

However, the question is not, "How can I eat like this for the rest of my life?" Rather, it should be, "How can I *not* eat like this for the rest of my life?" Let's face it: What you've been doing until now has paid off only in pain. Drastic steps must be taken to correct a drastic problem. That's why it is desirable not only to lose weight, but also to remove yourself forever from the love of foods that do you harm. The Rice Diet is an invaluable tool in accomplishing this objective.

Follow the Rice Diet and, over a period of time, you will lose your taste for the foods you once loved. You will still love and enjoy food, but you will come to prefer the delicious, nutritious foods that you're allowed. I assure you that plain, natural food is *sublime*.

Give yourself time, and you will come to love these new foods every bit as much as the destructive foods you used to eat. By working to retrain your tastes and inclinations, you *can* have the pleasures of food without the pain.

CHAPTER TEN

The Exercise Program

ON THE Rice Diet, if there is no medical contraindication, patients are instructed to lead normal, active lives. We are encouraged to exercise to the point of *maximum tolerance*. This varies with the person, of course, and depends on the age, sex, and health of the individual.

In general, the key is *get moving* and *stay* moving: With exercise, as with anything else, it's *consistency* that counts.

Exercise burns calories and fat while it works to build muscle. It increases the ratio of lean muscle tissue to fat tissue, which means you can weigh more yet look lean. Exercise improves heart and lung capacity, it gives your muscles tone and shape, and, best of all, it provides you with a general sense of well-being.

You will burn your food more efficiently if you raise your level of activity. When you exercise for a sustained period of time, you alter your metabolic rate, use up calories, and lose inches.

As a bonus, exercise inhibits appetite and helps control hunger. It helps you unwind and elevates your mood.

THE RIGHT PROGRAM FOR YOU

If you're not already engaged in an exercise program, you'll want to develop an individualized routine that takes into consideration your level of fitness, any health problems you may have, your interests, and your goals. As usual, you should check with your doctor first and listen to his or her advice.

Most find that some form of aerobic exercise suits their

129

needs best. Aerobic exercises include walking, running, cycling, and swimming. Yoga is another good choice. It gives you a total-body workout and relieves stress at the same time.

On the Rice Diet, all of the above forms of exercise are acceptable, with walking being the exercise most frequently recommended.

WHY WALKING?

Walking is a terrific and enjoyable exercise. It promotes all-over physical fitness and can be done anywhere, any time, and in all kinds of weather. It gives you the workout you need, and apart from shoes, it doesn't cost a dime.

It is a quick cure for mild depression, and it relieves tension and anxiety. By steadying your breathing and your heart rate, walking leaves you feeling more relaxed. It serves well to divert your attention from food, and it's good for your body, your mind, and even your social life!

If walking is the form of exercise that you select, the following hints might be helpful.

- Don't worry about how fast you're going. Walk quickly enough to make yourself breathe hard and work up a sweat, but not so fast that you're uncomfortable or completely out of breath.
- Try for a walking speed of 20 to 30 minutes per mile. If time is no problem, aim at 2 to 3 hours of walking per day. Naturally, this can be broken up into several separate periods during the day.
- Consider buying a pedometer, to keep an eye on your daily progress.
- If you want to increase your pace, alternate walking with jogging.
- Make profitable use of your time by thinking things over as you walk. Many dieters have discovered that walking generates solutions to whatever problems are on their

minds. You might even want to take a notepad along with you, should you have some ideas you want to jot down.

- Walk through different parts of town, so boredom won't become a problem. Look in store windows or compare architectural styles. If you feel comfortable with it, stop to chat with friendly strangers or to play with a neighborhood dog.

Perhaps you decide that walking is not for you. No problem—on the contrary, it's important not to force yourself to do anything you don't like. If you're not happy, you'll never stick with it.

There is a large variety of sports and exercise programs available, and you should investigate thoroughly to find one that suits your temperament and needs. Just be sure to select an activity that uses muscles in all parts of your body, something that will raise your pulse rate and make you work up a sweat.

SLOW, SAFE, AND REASONABLE

When you're beginning an exercise program, it is important to build up gradually. Take care not to overexert or overextend yourself. It's okay to get a little tired, but not exhausted.

It is natural to feel a little sore after a good workout. Indeed, it's a sign that your muscles are responding as they should. But don't try to take on too much too soon—you risk getting either injured or discouraged. It's far better to start off slowly and proceed at a comfortable pace. Fatigue or pain is an indication that you're doing too much.

Be sure to avoid all movements that cause you discomfort, particularly in or near joints. Watch out for nausea, hot or cold flashes, dizziness, and extreme breathlessness. Don't push yourself so hard that you won't want to resume your exercise program the next day. The guideline here is *be reasonable and consistent.*

Have you noticed how often the word "reasonable" surfaces in this book? As with your diet, it's important not to have an all-or-nothing approach to exercise. Anything is better than nothing, even walking up one small flight of stairs or standing on one foot while going up in an elevator. Work *something* in your body.

Start where you're comfortable, doing something that you find pleasant, something that *appeals* to you. Then work at increasing the time and effort you expend. Establish a realistic exercise schedule and stick to it as best as you can. Select the time of day that best fits your life-style, and don't throw in the towel if you miss a few days from time to time.

Even those with no confidence at all in their athletic ability will find that they can develop and improve over time. You just have to work at making the most of what you have.

Be sure to keep your expectations realistic, too. Do not expect remarkable changes in just a couple of weeks, although even within that short a space of time, you are likely to notice that you have more vitality and that there's some improvement in muscle tone.

MISCELLANEOUS EXERCISE TIPS

- Vary your routine to prevent boredom. If you walk one day, try bicycling the next. Do yoga on the third day and take an aerobics class on the fourth. Variety will help you retain your interest in continuing.
- Exercise to music.
- It helps alleviate boredom if you walk or work out with a friend.
- Consider team sports, which are fun, but only if you know you won't spend the majority of your time on the sidelines, kibitzing and not getting much exercise.
- Check out the various exercise classes offered in your area. Try to find one in which the other participants are at or about your level. If this proves difficult, ask the

instructors if it would be possible for them to individual-
ize the routines to meet your particular needs.

- On the subject of instructors, it is important that you make sure that the person in charge of your exercise class is adequately trained, in order to protect yourself from possible injury. Before joining any class, ask about the background, qualifications, and possible certification of the instructor.
- A treadmill stress test can be taken to determine your aerobic capacity. Ask your doctor if he or she thinks it would be advisable for you to have one.
- It's important to be physically comfortable when exercising. Wear loose clothing and properly fitted shoes.

Now push yourself . . . and _get moving!_

CHAPTER ELEVEN

The Time Element: How Long Will It Take?

THE FIRST question people ask me is, "How much weight did you lose?" Their second question is invariably, "And how long did it take?" Everyone wants to know what rate of weight loss can be expected.

Well, I'd like to be of help, but the truth is, this is an unanswerable question. There are simply too many unknowns and variables to take into account. Some are physiological in nature, and it is impossible to know how anyone's metabolism will perform. Factors such as age, gender, and activity level enter into the picture as well.

Not to mention the main variable: How often, and how badly, will you cheat?

Dr. Kempner pokes gentle fun at those who focus on how long it will take them to lose weight. He asks, "If a surgeon performs a delicate operation and saves a man's life, does it matter if the operation took two hours or four?" Or, "If a man makes ten million dollars, does it matter how long it took him to acquire the cash?"

In other words, it's only the end result that counts, not how long the achievement takes.

But as a fellow dieter, I can understand how important the time factor seems to you, so I'll attempt to shed some light on the subject.

First let's take a look at the issues involved.

GENDER DIFFERENCES

You've heard it before, now you're hearing it again. No matter *what* the diet, men tend to lose weight more quickly than women.

The chief physiological reason is that men have nearly twice the ratio of muscle to fat than do women. This means that they can work off calories in almost half the time.

In addition, female hormones work to turn food into fat. This may not seem "fair," but nature designed women this way so as to provide enough padding to protect a fetus during pregnancy. The fact that contemporary American women wouldn't appreciate this didn't count.

Some suggest that there are behavioral differences between men and women as well. Apparently, once a man initiates a diet program, he tends to adhere to it more strictly than a woman does.

I'd say that the fact that women are more often in contact with food doesn't help. As the ones who traditionally shop for, prepare, and serve meals to their families, women are more frequently exposed to food, which surely places their diets in greater jeopardy.

Menstruation can also cause women problems with their weight reduction programs. Alas, it can stimulate food cravings, especially for sweets. For some, this can begin a few days before their period arrives and last for ten to twelve days, until menstruation is through. In addition, menstruation frequently causes distressing emotional states (for example, depression), and this can also contribute to the desire to eat.

In recent years this monthly condition has been given a name—PMS, or Pre-Menstrual Syndrome—and it appears that a great many women suffer its consequences in one form or another.

In my case, five days before my period, I suddenly start craving sweets. Until that craving passes in a few hours or, at most, in a day, I am caught up in a frenzy of binging on junk food. I have found that the vegetarian-formula vitamins I mentioned in Chapter 7 seem to help. Since I've been taking them, my symptoms are far less severe. If PMS is a problem for you, you may want to investigate them or discuss them with your physician.

AGE

Though you commonly hear people say that they lose weight more slowly as they age, studies do not seem to bear out this theory.

What often *does* change with age, however, is your level of activity. If you think that your metabolism has slowed down over the years, you might try increasing the amount of exercise that you do.

An additional point to address here is the controversial question of whether you should weigh more or less as you age. Most medical practitioners agree with Dr. Kempner (who, at eighty-three, is 5'8" tall and weighs 134 pounds). He puts it this way. Say you have an eighty-year-old man and a twenty-year-old man. Before them stand an eighty-pound valise and a twenty-pound valise. Which man should carry which valise?

Right you are! Obviously the younger man is in a better position to carry somewhat more weight than the older man is. The moral: Cut down on your intake and your weight as you age. The lighter you are, the healthier you're likely to be, and remain.

ACTIVITY LEVEL

Activity alone will not cause you to lose weight, but when combined with a diet, it can produce a somewhat faster rate of loss. A consistent exercise program can stimulate your metabolic furnace to burn faster. Consider this: It's been said that Martina Navratilova burns up more calories just sitting in an armchair than you do playing tennis!

THE CRUCIAL ISSUE

Having discussed the factors that make a difference in weight loss, I'd now like to address the most critical issue of all: your attitude and your level of frustration about how long your weight loss takes.

Let's start with the very beginning of the diet.

For virtually all of you, the weight will come off very quickly at first. If you're a Group A dieter (an Almost-Thin), you'll see the change immediately, both on your scale and in the mirror. But those in Groups B and C (the Betweeners and Constant-Eaters) will have longer to wait for a *visible* change. Their losses *on the scale* are likely to be more impressive than those of Group A dieters, however, since the more overweight you are, the more quickly you tend to lose.

While a five- to ten-pound drop will be visible at once on someone who's only a few pounds overweight, the larger you are, the more weight you'll have to lose before anyone will notice. (On the bright side, however, as you approach your goal, each and every pound will show.)

Let me give you an illustration from my own experience.

After I had been in Durham for just over two months, my niece Amy came from Montreal to visit me. By then, I had lost 58½ pounds, going from 271½ to 213. A significant loss, to be sure, but I was still unquestionably fat. At the airport, Amy walked over to me, slowly looked me up and down, then reluctantly announced, "Welllll, maybe a little, in the face."

People are outraged when I recount this story, but after all, she was just telling the truth. I really didn't look much different from the Judy who had left Montreal. I had started out so fat that even a large drop in weight made no difference at all.

But wouldn't I have been foolish to have taken her comment to heart? It's understandable that you get discouraged, but what good does it do?

Interestingly, only a week after Amy's departure, there was a marked change in my appearance. Suddenly, everyone was telling me how much thinner I looked. And it was true.

One of my Ricer friends refers to this common phenomenon as "losing a layer," and that's exactly how it appears. You'll see a dieter's weight consistently going down, yet there's little or no difference immediately apparent on the body, where it counts. Then one day there's a shift, and a narrower, thinner person emerges. Everyone notices, and compliments flow.

I have watched this happen to virtually all people who reduce. The weight loss on the scale may be steady and gradual, but the manifestation of the loss is a sudden surprise.

But I'm reminding you, you in Groups B and C, that the beginning can be a discouraging time. You won't be getting reinforcement or gratification from any source at all. You'll be doing without the delights of food, but you won't yet have the pleasure of seeing yourself thin.

This is a time for patience, a time of waiting without reward. And we fat people are notoriously disinclined to put off our pleasures. Part of our problem is that we want what we want *now*.

Working at reducing is like stopping biting your nails. You don't acquire long, lovely nails the day after you desist. And it's the same with your body. Much as you wish it could be otherwise, your rate of progress is not under your control. But your diet *is*. And the weight loss will come if you see the diet through. It's important not to allow momentary disappointments to impel you to eat.

TEMPORARY DELAYS

There are three main kinds of setbacks you can expect to encounter on your road, and these are discussed below.

Gains caused by binges. There's a great deal to be said

about this common occurrence. I go into detail on the subject in Chapter 14.

Briefly staying the same, or small, undeserved gains.
Occasionally there are days when your weight stays the same or unaccountably goes up, despite the fact that you've been following the diet without transgression.

I have heard people roar in pain if they haven't lost any weight after a good day of dieting, or if they show a gain. They insist that this is *not fair,* and almost demand some kind of accounting!

Normally, of course, a diet day is followed by a loss, but there are definitely times when this is just not the case. Like it or not, it is a reality you must accept.

My advice is to get over your disappointment as quickly as possible (about one minute seems appropriate), then get on with your day. Don't become dispirited or allow the number on the scale to affect your mood. Don't compare yourself with others on the diet, and don't waste time or energy bemoaning your failure to lose.

In my case, there were many days when I stayed the same, and an average of five or six times a month when my weight actually went up. I learned that there was simply no point in protesting metabolic facts of life. No matter how perfect our diet, our bodies are subject to random variations.

I suggest that you find some enjoyable way of spending your time, and stop worrying about the number on the scale. Stay on the diet and, I promise you, the weight will come off. If you allow setbacks to deter you, you won't stand a chance.

Plateaus. The bane of a dieter's existence, plateaus are frustrating times that most of us know well—periods when a week or more can go by without offering up a loss. Though infrequent on the Rice Diet, they nonetheless can occur. My advice remains the same: Keep your eye on your goal. See all obstacles through. Remind yourself that no other diet (short of a complete fast, perhaps) provides a quicker weight loss. Even with the occasional plateau, your overall loss will be so fast that it shouldn't be hard to stay motivated.

In my case, I had only one period I would call a plateau. It occurred as I hovered just above 200 pounds, and it lasted about a week. I have since learned from the Rice House staff that this is a fairly common plateau area. It's as if there's some underlying reluctance about getting into a ''normal'' range.

I also had difficulty getting out of the 130s, but this did not fall into the category of a ''plateau.'' After I lost my initial 140 pounds, it was over two years before I continued on toward goal. Essentially, I stopped dieting *to lose* at this time, though this was certainly not a conscious decision on my part. I still followed Rice Diet guidelines and I continued eating most of my meals at the Rice House, but I was not good about limiting the quantities I ate, nor did I eat only permissible foods. I was thin, and I maintained my loss, but I was obviously not ready to complete the job at that point. But never did I abandon my ultimate goal.

You too may reach a weight that you consciously or unconsciously choose to stay at for a lengthy period of time. No harm done, as long as you maintain your loss and as long as you realize where you eventually must head.

PLATEAU STRATEGIES

If you are on a genuine plateau (a minimum of one week without any loss at all), there are certain ''shock'' tactics that might stimulate your body to move. Rice and fruit are usually effective, or you might try one of the following for *one day only.*

Grapefruit

Use grapefruit juice, fresh grapefruit, and/or canned grapefruit segments. Have one portion for breakfast, three portions for lunch, and three portions for dinner. You may have less if you wish, but not more. Permissible noncaloric beverages are allowed. (See the list in Chapter 7.) One portion consists of 1 cup of unsweetened juice, or half a fresh grapefruit, or 1 cup of sweetened segments, including 2 tablespoons of juice. Mix and match, as you prefer.

Tomatoes, Eggs, and Grapefruit

Half a grapefruit for breakfast; one sliced tomato, one egg, and half a grapefruit at lunch and again at dinner. Be sure to deduct this from your egg allotment for the week. Permissible noncaloric beverages are allowed. One cup of unsweetened grapefruit juice or 1 cup of sweetened grapefruit segments (including 2 tablespoons of juice) may be substituted for the fresh half grapefruit at any meal.

Note: This should not be undertaken by anyone with medical problems, not even for a day.

A Total Fast

One day of any of the above alternatives should jolt you off your plateau. But they are certainly not necessary. If you keep following the Rice Diet as written, within very short order you can expect to start losing weight again.

Overall, it's important to take a positive approach to delays. Look at how much you've accomplished, not at how far you still have to go. And acknowledge that no matter *how* fast you lose, it still won't be fast enough to suit you. Like all dieters I know, you'd really like to be thin by tomorrow morning, at the latest!

QUICK VERSUS SLOW LOSS

I have sometimes heard it argued that if you lose weight quickly, you risk putting it back on quickly, whereas if you lose more slowly, it improves your chances of keeping it off. A nice theory but it has not been my experience.

I once lost weight *very* slowly with a well-known diet organization. But when I went off the diet, I sure put it on fast. Indeed, in the first week, I put on twelve pounds, and in the second week, eight—only a few days to put on weight it had taken me four months to lose

Dieting is hard, whether you're on a diet that takes off weight quickly or slowly. Either you're emotionally ready to be thin or you're not. And if you *are,* then why not lose the weight as quickly as you can? Deprivation is deprivation—it might as well pay off.

"BY THE DAY OF DEBBIE'S WEDDING . . ."

I have one last recommendation to make on the subject of time.

I strongly suggest you stop "deciding" or "resolving" to be a certain weight by a certain date. Such projections are nothing more than daydreams and wishful thinking. Indeed, to call them nonsense is not pushing it too far.

Now tell the truth. How many times have you given yourself a deadline, and when have you ended up where you vowed that you'd be? Yeah, I know. Me too.

It is pointless, even harmful, to set goals that lock you into being a particular weight by a given date. You're putting unnecessary pressure on yourself, and you're setting yourself up for failure as well. Your goal should remain steadfast, but the timing of it is simply not under your control.

I understand that you want to be thin as soon as possible, but the emphasis here should be on "possible," not "soon." It is unrealistic to think you can map your progress ahead of time. Unfortunately, there will be many unplanned turns along the way. (Do you think for a minute I planned to stop at 130 for *two years?*)

Stop projecting the outcome—just take the first step and

do your best each day. Keep your mind on your goal, and let time do the rest.

Learn to appreciate that a *good diet day* is more important than the number you see on the scale. It will make you feel better physically. It will contribute to your self-respect. And eventually it will lead you to reaching your goal. Each individual day's *weight* does not matter. At all.

CHAPTER TWELVE

Three Major Guidelines

THERE ARE three main principles that are so crucial that I do not believe one can have long-term success on a diet without eventually internalizing them. They are philosophical in nature, they require daily attention and they call for thought and permanent change.

Because of their importance, I would like to go into some detail.

GUIDELINE 1: WORK HARD AT DISTANCING YOURSELF FROM AN INAPPROPRIATE LOVE OF FOOD

It is to your advantage to stop loving foods that are bad for you. To the extent that you indulge your senses (*all* your senses) in the love and appreciation of food, you will have trouble remaining on a diet. It is impossible for a person who loves food to look at it, hear about it, smell it, read about it, or discuss it without eventually succumbing to the inevitable temptation to eat it.

If you're at all like me, *anything* to do with food can set you off. I remember a couple I used to see in marriage counseling. Every week the man had a new complaint to air, and he invariably used the expression "cheesed off" to express his irritation. He was "cheesed off" with his wife for doing this; he was "cheesed off" with her for doing that. I don't have to tell you how hard it was for me to keep my mind on the session after I heard those words!

Cheese, which I had not even been thinking of, now surged to the forefront of my mind. It was all I could do to pay attention to anything either of them said. All I could think of was, "How much longer is this session going to last? I've got to get out of here and get myself some cheese."

People with weight problems are simply too vulnerable to food cues to expose themselves to them any more than is absolutely necessary. Dieting is a matter of thought, speech, and action, and the desire for food must be attacked on all three of these levels. Avoid exposing yourself to food or food cues in any form or guise. You should avoid even the *topic* of food.

More important than controlling your diet is controlling your mind. It is your *thoughts* about food that are causing you to eat. Happily, thoughts can be controlled. I therefore offer the following suggestions:

Don't read restaurant reviews or the food columns that appear in your newspaper.

Don't read the menu in a restaurant. You know perfectly well what you can have. Why read enticing descriptions of what you *can't* have?

Do not read recipes. You might even want to cut out women's magazines altogether while you're on the diet. Their full-color spreads are designed to make your mouth water. Not to mention the food ads!

Of course, TV ads for food are even worse than those in print. It's almost as if the food is right there before you. Some of it can even be ordered in the time it takes to make a phone call! The purpose of these ads is to provoke you into eating whatever they are advertising. Admit it—you hadn't even been thinking of food when that ad came on, and now you absolutely must have it.

Since it's hard to avoid ads that crop up during a program you're watching, I suggest you alter the color controls on your television to turn it into a black-and-white set. It's amazing how much less tantalizing food is in black and white. Sometimes you'll have a hard time even distinguishing what it is!

More important than any of the above: *Stop talking about food.* I cannot overstate how important I believe this to be.

Many of the patients at the Rice House spend their meal-times talking about food: what they wish they were eating, what's the first thing they're going to eat as soon as they get home, where to get the best whatever, what their favorite foods are, etc. How can anyone hear food extolled and rhapsodized about in such loving and lyrical fashion without longing to dig right in? And you know how often wanting to eat leads to actually eating. Limiting your intake is much easier if you don't first arouse your desire for food. It is far easier to *avoid* temptation than to work at overcoming it.

It is also important not to listen to others talk about food. I remember the time a Ricer friend went on and on for two solid weeks about two particular binge items she was longing to eat. At the end of the two weeks, *I* went out and ate them! Moreover, these were foods that I would never normally choose!

You will, of course, frequently find yourself in the company of people who are discussing food. What should you do? Easy. Try tuning them out, and if you can't, change the topic. If need be, walk away to "get yourself a glass of water."

Some of you may protest that it is "not fattening" to look at, hear about, or read about food. You don't see why you can't continue this noncaloric relationship with your beloved food. This is missing the point. It is foolhardy to continually expose yourself to things you want but cannot have. It can only increase your desires and weaken your resolve. More often than not, thoughts do lead to action.

Yes, I know. It's very hard to give something up totally when you love it so much. And that's why it's crucial to work at stopping loving food the way you do. If you can learn to love it less (and you can), cutting down will be less painful.

If you allow yourself to continue your loving attachment to food, I believe that ultimately you stand little chance of losing weight. It is only a question of time until you eat.

You are causing yourself much suffering by building up desires that cannot be satisfied. The only way to find *real* satisfaction is to stop desiring what is beyond your reach.

GUIDELINE 2: LEARN TO LOVE THE FOODS YOU *CAN* HAVE

The bleak prospect suggested by the foregoing section is that never again can you enjoy the unquestionable pleasures of food. Wrong! In fact, nothing could be farther from the truth.

You can still love food, each and every mouthful. And you can even approximate that heavenly prospect of "eating all you want of the foods you love without gaining an ounce."

If you learn to love the foods that you are allowed to eat.

This is a simple, obvious, and very basic truth. Rather than create in yourself the desire for the foods you cannot have, why not work at appreciating the many delicious and healthy foods that *are* available to you?

You think this is hard? Not so. But it does require effort, application, and time, as does everything else worth having in this life.

And just think of the payoff! You'll get to eat lots of the foods you love without jeopardizing your health or your figure. How much easier it is to stick to a diet if you look forward to every meal, enjoy each bite, and feel happy and satisfied at the end. This is obviously the perfect solution for those who want to be thin but don't want to give up the delights of food.

Even though I still love food as much as I ever did, it is now Rice Diet-type foods that I actually prefer, not any of the foods I used to eat when I was fat. I still occasionally get in the mood for junk, but it certainly doesn't tempt me on a daily basis. I have a far more pleasurable experience eating pure and healthy food, and everything I now eat tastes absolutely delicious to me.

I may still want excessive quantities (some things never change), but now I want excessive quantities of *good* food, not junk.

"But wait!" I hear you say. "You mean I can never again eat ice cream, cake, or any of my favorites?"

Well, yes and no. Yes, on occasion (because the truth is that you will occasionally choose to eat those foods). But no, not as a way of life. Not if you're wise, and if you want the best possible life for yourself.

Just as God made sex enjoyable so that man would indulge and procreate, in the same way He made food tasty so that man would eat it and survive. We got out of the habit of eating plain, unadulterated food long ago, and over the years, we have become accustomed to increasingly processed and tampered-with food. No wonder food in its natural state seems bland and tasteless to us now!

Remember that your taste buds have been dulled by the flavorings and additives found in most foods. Once you wean yourself from doctored foods (and the Rice Diet is very effective in accomplishing this, given time), I assure you that you will come to *prefer* the plainest preparation of food. *You will come to enjoy it as much as you enjoy the foods you now eat.*

I now eat a plain baked potato with as much relish as when I dolloped butter and sour cream over it. And a plain ear of corn tastes better to me now than one saturated with butter and salt. Nor do I want my apple mixed into a "Betty," a "Charlotte," or a "crisp." A plain tart and crunchy apple will suit me just fine, thank you. And though plain food gives me pleasure, it does not entice me to overdo.

Please note: *It took time for me to reach this point.*

And it will take you a concerted effort over a long period of time for this new approach to food to become automatic. But it is worth it—and if you want to be thin, what alternative do you have?

It is easier to be happy in life if you focus on what is available to you, instead of concentrating on what you lack. Forget about what's missing; look at what is there.

If you cannot control your desires, you will constantly feel frustrated, resentful, and angry. There can be no peace of mind for those who are acutely aware of what they don't have.

Wanting foods that are bad for you is inevitably a no-win situation. Either you want them and don't have them, in which case you feel deprived, or you want them and *do* have them, in which case you hate yourself and remain fat. Isn't it better to learn not to want them at all? Isn't it better to learn to love the foods you can have?

But please don't expect this changeover in your desires to take place at once. It is a process, not a single decision you can make. But with time and the feelings of well-being generated by proper eating, you will gradually, almost automatically, arrive at this goal. You need only enter the process with an attitude of willingness and cooperation. As you slowly internalize the knowledge that bad food makes you physically and emotionally miserable, you will *choose* to opt for proper nutrition—and joy.

GUIDELINE 3: BEHAVE IN WAYS THAT YOU BELIEVE TO BE ETHICALLY AND MORALLY RIGHT

This may seem like a most unusual suggestion to find in a diet book, but it is central to what I believe to be the only effective approach to permanent weight loss.

Becoming your best self, making your life better, cannot be approached along only one line—your body, your weight. It can work only as part of an overall plan, a commitment to making yourself the best you can be.

The past fifteen years have seen an explosion of self-help books, all dedicated to showing us how to be our best. What this generally means is being slim, fit, assertive, self-confident—all the buzzwords of our times. I have not seen any books that exhort us to be our *ethical* best, yet surely this deserves equal emphasis in any effort to improve ourselves and our lives.

I am not talking about major humanitarian gestures, but rather about the many small moments that make up our day. Essentially, we should try to live each moment with the greater good in mind (always remembering that we're human and have many flaws).

Try adopting small behaviors that make you feel good about yourself.

For example, if at heart you believe it's not right to litter, yet you throw Kleenex or paper out of the car window. . . . Well, it's not a terrible crime, but each time you do it chips off a little piece.

Or say you know you should offer an elderly lady your seat on a crowded bus, but you feel like sitting yourself, so you avert your eyes and stay where you are. Again, not a major offense, but you're sure not going to feel as good about yourself as you would if you stood and offered her your seat.

Other suggestions (among the many thousands of possibilities):

- Say please, thank you, and excuse me. Behave courteously and responsibly toward others.
- If you agree to do something, do it to the best of your ability. Don't be lazy about doing things the way you know they should be done.
- When you feel unhappy and deprived, think of what you can do for someone else. Doing a good deed, showing love to someone who's needy, will make you feel so good that you wouldn't dream of causing yourself pain by eating. As always, the love you give to others will help *you*.
- In general, try to act with decency, manners, and consideration. Such behavior cannot help but make you feel better about yourself. And if you do it consistently, you will replace self-hatred with self-respect. Remember, while it is true that losing weight leads to self-respect, it is equally true that self-respect leads to losing weight.

We hear a lot these days about the importance of self-esteem, but very little about applying moral concepts to the acquisition of this desirable trait. Popular psychology likes to lay the development (or lack of development) of self-esteem at our parents' door. Apparently, if we did not get what we needed from them during our formative years, we are subject to lifelong problems with our perception of ourselves. Perhaps so, but where does that leave us? Either struggling interminably in therapy or denying responsibility for whatever happens in our lives.

I prefer the term "self-respect" to the fashionable (and elusive) "self-esteem." And happily, self-respect is downright easy to build up. All we have to do is behave in ways that we respect ourselves for.

Please note that I am not referring to ethical and moral behavior as defined and commanded by others. I am not for a moment suggesting that you do what other people think you "should."

No, I am referring to your own strong inner moral code, the behaviors you believe at heart to be ethically and morally right.

We all have our own standards for correct behavior. If we don't observe those standards and don't live in ways that are consistent with what we believe to be right, we are separated from our best selves. To the extent that we can make our behavior match our beliefs, we will foster self-respect, self-esteem, and their accompanying rewards.

Rise above yourself. Behave in ways that you approve of. Try to be the best that you can be.

Do you at heart think a little less of yourself because you often pull into work late? Or because you pilfer small items from the office? Or pad your expense account? Stop doing it. I assure you, the rewards will accrue to *you.*

If how you behave is different from how you (really) believe you should behave, you are a house divided and you cannot be at peace. You are lacking the inner-outer consistency that you require to feel content.

Look closely and sincerely at what you do and at what you leave undone. It may appear difficult to do what is right, but believe me, it is easier than doing what you know is wrong. Inevitably, to harm others is to profoundly harm yourself.

I like the motto "Go through life helpful and harmless"—a brief sentence, but it encompasses thousands of behaviors. Not one day goes by that we don't have many opportunities to be both. When in doubt, ask yourself how *you* would feel about something, or what *you* would want in a given situation.

Inwardly, we all long to be our best selves. Getting our bodies in shape is just one aspect of that quest. We know that when we're at our best, we're also the happiest. To seek happiness in life is to seek endlessly and in vain. But if we fulfill our need to be our best, in each and every way, happiness will result.

Those multiple small "good feelings" that you get when you behave ethically and morally cannot be overestimated. They give you an overall positive feeling, a perception of yourself as a good and decent person.

That kind of feeling permits you to do all sorts of nice things for yourself, including losing weight. How you nourish your inner self will be reflected in how you nourish your outer self. It is no accident that an epidemic of weight problems is taking place in an era that encourages the "Me Generation" to "do your own thing."

Be your best in *every* way and see what happens to your weight!

CHAPTER THIRTEEN
Miscellaneous Tips

DIETING IS a serious undertaking, and any techniques we can find to smooth our path are sure to be welcome. The following tips, suggestions, and how-to's have all been of help to me at various times, and I'm sure many of them will be useful to you as well.

DIETARY TACTICS

- If you're female, and it's close to your period, you might consider waiting until your period is over before beginning the diet. Many women crave sweets before and/or during their period, and you might give yourself a better start by avoiding this additional stress.
- For no discernible reason, there are days when we're hungry and days when we're not. I believe in taking advantage of those not-so-hungry days by eating lightly. This also allows me to feel comfortable about eating somewhat more on those days when I'm unaccountably a little hungrier than usual.
- Sometimes I have a really hard time with food, and my mechanisms of control are not very strong. At those times, I acknowledge that I can't deal with both quality and quantity right now, and I decide to relax my vigilance about *how much* I eat.

   This means I allow myself all I want of one nondamaging category of food, either fruit or vegetables. As long as I eat nothing else, I permit myself to eat all the fruit or vegetables I want. One or two days of this kind of eating always gets my appetite back under control, and I can then return to my regular phase without problems.

- When I find that I am reacquiring too much of a love for food (thinking about it a lot, salivating over upcoming meals, etc.), I try to go back on rice and fruit for a few days. This effectively makes me lose interest in food, while at the same time offering me nourishing and satisfying meals. I thus use rice and fruit as much to control my appetite as to lose or maintain my weight.

  I recommend the rice and fruit regimen because it leaves no questions unanswered, no room to maneuver and make mistakes. It is two fruit portions and a bowl of rice, period. Zucchini may be low in calories, but portioning it out leaves room for decision and choice, and there are times when I'm fragile and can't be counted on to do that wisely. Rice and fruit take all such decision making out of my hands. The worst damage I can do is to buy myself the biggest fruit I can find. But a banana is still a banana, and I'd be hard put to get more than an extra 20 or 30 calories out of even the largest banana I could find.

- There are other possible applications of rice and fruit meals:

  1. Consider one day of rice and fruit each week after you're past Phase I—even (especially) once you're on Maintenance. Should you decide to do this, I'd recommend Monday as the best day. The weekend is over and few events are scheduled on Mondays.

  2. Fruit and rice lunches are filling and low-calorie. They are particularly enjoyable in spring and summer, when so much delicious fruit is available. And they will speed along your diet progress, whatever phase you're on.

  3. If you have an eating occasion coming up (party, vacation, etc.), you might try eating only fruit and rice for a few days in advance. This will reduce your appetite and make overindulgence less likely. Moreover, you'll gravitate more toward vegetables than toward sweets.

- Ask yourself before you eat, "How hungry am I right now?" then try to eat accordingly. Don't put any food on your plate until you've answered that question. Most of the time, we unthinkingly eat whatever is put in front of us. If you ascertain in advance that at this particular moment you're not really very hungry, you can often choose to eat less. Instead of eating mechanically, you'll be acting with awareness.

- Ideally, you should have no nonpermissible foods in the house while you are on the diet. Throw them away or give them away. While in Durham, I never even kept my fridge plugged in!

- Keep a stock of tomato sauce in the house, frozen into separate portion-sized containers. It is good over rice or mixed with baked onions, eggplant, or zucchini. It is great as a sauce over fish, chicken, or eggs, and it also works well as a base for delicious soups. All this for about 50 calories a cup.

- I have a microwave so that I can eat what I want when I want it. I'm too fragile to play John Wayne with food. Maybe I'm not a hero, but keeping the proper foods as accessible as possible helps me stay thin.

- The way you eat food can have an inexplicable effect on how satisfying it is. I used to like to eat baked potatoes out of my hand, like apples. Unfortunately, it sometimes took three or four potatoes until I began to feel full. Yet I find *one* potato, eaten with a fork and knife, both filling and satisfying.

  You might experiment along these lines with various foods. Try slicing your bananas or apples into a bowl, grating or shredding your vegetables, etc. See what works for you.

- Dieters are always being advised to eat more slowly, and I second that advice. The reason usually given is that it takes 20 minutes for food to reach your bloodstream, thus letting you know that you're full. By eating quickly, you take in more food than you really need.

  In addition, it is downright unappetizing to watch people cram in food in massive bites. To see someone demolish a banana in three bites is (almost!) enough to make you lose your own appetite. Proper eating manners cannot help but add to your sense of self-respect, just as slovenly habits are sure to diminish it.

- When a particular food keeps entering your mind and you're in imminent danger of eating it, a last resort is to visualize having it in your mouth. Truly taste each imaginary bite, keeping aware of both texture and taste. Although I believe you are far wiser to turn your attention away from food when feeling tempted, there are times when that just doesn't work. Sometimes, "as if" experiences can prevent you from giving in to the real thing. Why eat it (and gain weight) if you can virtually taste it without putting it in your mouth?

- Occasionally you may feel dizzy on the diet, especially on very hot days or if you change position abruptly. If this condition persists, speak to your doctor and consider the temporary addition of a little salt to your diet. At the Rice House, we are given 2 ounces of tomato juice or a slice of regular bread to meet this infrequent need.

ACTIVITIES

- Nurturing is a key word. While dieting, be as good to yourself as you can. Invest as much time and money as you can afford in making yourself feel good. Since you cannot reward yourself with food, reward yourself in other ways. Have massages, facials, manicures, etc. If it helps you get thin, it's worth whatever it costs. (And I'll bet those luxuries will cost you less than you used to squander on food!) If money is a problem, treat yourself to a new color of nail polish or a pair of patterned panty hose.

- Keep busy and active. Do what gives you peace and pleasure. Don't rush off and do calisthenics if that isn't what you enjoy. If it makes you happy to sit at home watching TV, then that is what you should be doing. The rule of thumb is: Spend as much time as possible doing the things you enjoy and as little time as possible doing the things you don't like to do.

- Eliminate as many of the stresses in your life as you can. Dieting is hard work, and no one can handle too many pressures at once. Some suggestions: Slow down your pace, stop rushing. You may think that pushing yourself helps you accomplish more, but if the stress affects your peace of mind, it will invariably affect your ability to diet. Avoid situations that will make you crave the solace of food.

- Transition periods can be difficult—those times when you're changing from one activity to the next (e.g., when you arrive home after work, or right after dinner). When time hangs heavy on your hands, you feel restless and have fitful thoughts about food. It is important that you be prepared for these times. If you're a reader, always have several books out of the library, to be sure that at least one of them will hold your interest. Consider timing your arrival home to coincide with a TV program you enjoy. Make sure you have access to several pleasurable alternatives to cope with these times of particular stress.

- The next time you're at the library, look under "Reducing" to see what resources are available. Over the past few years, many interesting books about dieting and binging have been published. By consulting them, you can pick up a variety of useful insights and tips.

- Find ways to be happy, things to be happy about. If you don't even notice the many sources of happiness in your life, how can you enjoy them? I therefore suggest that at least once a day you take the time to count your blessings. It's important to be aware of how many things are *good* in your life. People with food problems often concentrate on these problems to the exclusion of all else, and this is truly a sad way of going through life.

- If you're a believer, I suggest you ask God every morning for a good diet day, and thank Him each night for whatever measure of success you've had. Ask His help whenever you feel like overeating. Pray for food to become unimportant to you. Pray for peace about food, diet, and weight issues. Before each meal, I say a short prayer in which I thank the Lord for the delicious, nutritious food before me and ask Him to help me eat whatever I require to meet my needs and help me stop eating as soon as my needs have been met. This works!

- Even before you're ready to buy new clothes, I suggest you go into the stores to see what's available and try things on. Try on clothes you're not used to wearing, even if you're convinced that you won't look good in them because they're "not your style." Keep an open mind. This is a new you you're unveiling!

- You may be tempted to keep wearing your clothes long after they're too big. Perhaps you're figuring that you're losing weight so quickly, there's no point in spending money on clothes that won't fit in a couple of weeks. An understandable sentiment; nonetheless I recommend that you allot yourself a small monthly clothing budget. It is encouraging, while dieting, to look as good as you can, and baggy pants aren't going to do it for you. I allowed myself $50 a month (which included whatever alterations I needed), and I shopped mostly Goodwill. That was good enough for the time being, and it gave me some of the pleasure of new clothes. (And no, I do not believe in hanging on to your fat clothes "just in case"!)

- Consult a trained color analyst and "get your colors done." This process identifies you as a "spring," "summer," "winter," or "fall," and suggests a palette of colors best suited to your skin tone. It's fun, it helps you plan your wardrobe, and it's constructive encouragement to get thin.

- A suggestion for those entrepreneurially inclined: In the Raleigh-Durham area there are some enterprising ladies who prepare and deliver diet meals to dieters. If there is a sizable contingent of dieters in your area, this might be a way for some of you to earn extra money while helping others.

RELATIONSHIPS

- Find a doctor you like on a personal level, someone who is responsive and understanding, someone you'll enjoy reporting to and trying to please. Ideally, you and your doctor should have a relationship in which you work together toward your goal.
- I think it's time for overweight people to come out of the closet. Even people who *used* to be overweight don't want anyone to know it, as if some heinous crime is buried in their past. But to have been overweight and to have conquered it is surely an achievement. Without going on obsessively about your weight, learn to discuss your food issues with the people closest to you. Include your friends and family in your thoughts, concerns, and plans. Don't expect them to take responsibility for your behavior or to become your caretaker, but do let them help you through therapeutic sharing.
- Is there someone in your house who is "helping" you by hiding foods you can't have? I know of instances where wives have been hiding food—and husbands routinely finding it—daily for over thirty years! To my mind, these are sick games that do no one any good. If unpermitted foods must be in the house (and I question this), I recommend a locked cupboard to which all family members but the dieter have the key. I'm not fond of this solution, but at least it's an honest and up-front approach.
- Don't listen to other dieters. It goes without saying that you should *never* take diet advice from anyone who doesn't have his or her own eating under control. Everyone thinks they know what others should do to lose weight, and usually they're only too happy to tell you. Thank them, but tune them out. This is an area where even the experts are in the dark. Unless the source of advice has demonstrated success in dieting, you'd be well advised to disregard what he or she says, no matter how well meant.

- By all means, use the "buddy system" and go on this diet with a friend. However, do not tie your actual intake to what the other person chooses to eat. In other words, "Let's start the Rice Diet together" is fine, but "Let's eat nothing but grapefruit tomorrow" is not recommended. You should both be free to choose what appeals to you, whatever will make you feel happier and more satisfied. This will also eliminate the "Well, Mary broke her diet, so I might as well break mine" school of thought.
- Spend as much of your time as possible with people whose company you enjoy and who make you feel good about yourself. Spend as little time as possible with those who leave you with bad feelings.
- I find it helps both my diet and my life if I go out looking my best. I am less interested in eating when I look good, partly because interesting things seem to happen more frequently then. I relate differently to people, and they react differently to me. When you look good, you feel good, and your demeanor is more inviting.

Outlook

- "MYSELF FIRST. NOT *ONLY*, BUT FIRST." Your primary goal must be to lose weight. And to get results, your diet and your needs have to come first. This is not a selfish perspective if you bear the above motto in mind. And remember, *everyone* in your life will benefit if you lose weight and feel wonderful.
- Keep a wise check on your emotions. Some examples:

  Pick and choose what you get angry about. If something isn't really that important, let it go. You may feel that you are thus sparing someone who deserves to be told off, but face it—the one who gets riled and upset is *you*.

  Worry appropriately. If something happening in your life *this very minute* seems to call for worry, then go ahead. But most of our worries are about the future or the past. Don't focus on upcoming crises—try to live your life *now*. (To tell you the truth, that's all you've really got.)

• Avoid asking yourself any questions that start out with "Why":

"Why did I have that extra baked potato?"

"Why can't I stay on a diet?"

"Why am I so self-destructive?"

You cannot *know* why, so you might as well save your time and energy. Even if you do come up with some answer, you can't know for sure that you're right, so the whole thing is really an exercise in futility.

• Look in mirrors often and at length. Put judgment aside and look at your body with love. Forget the flabby thighs and the protruding belly—what's *good* about what you see? I am not talking about the different parts of your body, but about health and the use of your limbs. Count your blessings and love the good things you see. Learn to relax about your body. Accept your imperfections, faults, and flaws.

I overheard two women talking in the Rice House about a third patient, a woman who had lost over 200 pounds and was almost at goal. "Yes," said one woman to the other, "but she still has big hips." As if this invalidated her loss; as if it was almost not worth losing the weight if her body remained imperfect.

This episode reminded me of a recent study indicating what percentage of women disliked their breasts, what percentage disliked their thighs, etc. Imagine doing such a study! Yet women (more than men) commonly divide their bodies into pieces and comment critically on each separate part. What woman looks in the mirror without focusing on the areas she thinks should be improved?

I believe that we must find peace about our bodies because to hate our bodies is, bluntly, to hate ourselves. You may protest, "But my body isn't me." Well, let's face it, if your body goes to Connecticut, *you* go to Connecticut. And if your body feels hot, don't you feel hot, too?

Do the best you can do to get yourself in shape, then put self-criticism aside and enjoy life fully with the body you have. Your body doesn't have to be perfect, and most certainly, *you* do not have to be perfect. I do recommend, however, that you try to be your *best*.

- Losing weight should be part of an overall commitment to looking after yourself. Wear your seat belt, take your vitamins, don't take unnecessary chances, etc.

Miscellaneous

- Make your environment as peaceful as possible. Keep your living space clean, and decorate it in a warm and welcoming fashion. You spend a lot of time there. You should feel good about where you live.

  Listen to music that both soothes and pleases you. Avoid raucous, insistent beats while you're trying to diet. Keep away from traffic and noisy places. Drive more slowly. Take the phone off the hook when you're not feeling up to "putting out" for others.

  These are easy things to accomplish, and they're all part of being good to yourself.

- Cold seems to affect a great number of people, myself included. Keep your house or apartment at the temperature you like best. Try not to expose yourself to any unpleasant physical sensations (right down to minor things, like not wearing shoes that pinch).

- People with weight problems are sometimes lax about taking good care of themselves in general. Be sure to take care of all your physical needs. If you're tired, rest or go to sleep. If you have a headache, don't suffer, take an aspirin.

CHAPTER FOURTEEN

Binging: Before, During, and After

IN ALL THE diet books I've read (which is every diet book ever printed!), I have yet to see the subject of binging adequately addressed. Perhaps because these books are traditionally written by doctors, not by dieters, this area is neither acknowledged nor discussed. Yet obviously it is a matter of major concern.

The implication is that binges should never happen, that one should go on a diet and stick to it, without stopping, all the way to goal. This tends to reinforce the dieter's all-or-nothing belief that if a binge occurs, you are no longer on the diet. Anything short of the *perfect* diet is failure, and cause to throw in the towel. Far from assuring you of victory, however, this perfectionism only guarantees that you'll fail.

Let's call a spade a spade here. Hasn't food *always* been a difficult issue for you to deal with? Hasn't it posed a problem for many, many years? How could it be that all of a sudden, just because you've "decided" to go on a diet, all that's going to stop?

Unfortunately, your desire to eat will not leave you—not now and not ever. Your battles with food are, alas, destined to remain. That being the case, you'd best learn how to handle them.

Realize that no one can stick to a diet 100 percent without faltering. Occasional binges are inevitable. What's more, they can be enjoyed!

For true lovers of food, like you and me, it's virtually certain that at times we will succumb. Despite our best efforts, despite our genuine desire to lose weight.

163

And what's so terrible about that? Indeed, the occasional binge can be a delight. It has nothing to do with whether or not we become thin. We can have binges, learn to contain them, and still succeed in losing weight.

I can tell you that I binge routinely, and I know now that I always will. I rarely get through even two weeks without a fling. But I return to the diet, and it all works out.

Only those with a very small amount of weight to lose can undertake a diet confidently expecting never to cheat. They aren't going to be on it long enough to face the inevitable! The rest of us who need to diet for longer periods can be sure that our efforts will be punctuated with the intermittent lapse.

FROM SMUG TO SENSIBLE

Like most newcomers to Durham, I arrived feeling self-righteous and smug. I was astonished to discover that many of the dieters actually cheated. I couldn't understand it, and was positive *I* never would. Not me! Not our Judy! I was going straight to goal, with nary a pause along the way.

This agreeable fantasy lasted all of two weeks, at which point I ended up gorging on fast food. The reality, then as now, is that I'll always be capable of going berserk over food. Today I'm thin and I maintain my weight, but not a month goes by that I don't overindulge at least a couple of times.

For example, one night a few months ago, I was convinced that I just "had to" have ice cream. Though it was two o'clock in the morning, I drove to the supermarket and bought myself a quart. Then I sat in my car in the parking lot, gouging it out of the container *with a key!* I couldn't even wait to get home to eat it properly. After all, home was four minutes away. Who could possibly wait?

So don't look to *me* for advice about how never to cheat. I don't think it's possible, and I don't even aim for it anymore. I accept and *enjoy* the occasional binge. I know that it's inevitable—and not inconsistent with being thin.

One day a new arrival came up to me at the Rice House. She weighed over 300 pounds and obviously had severe problems with food. Yet she solemnly announced that she'd "decided" never again to eat sweets. Naturally, I wished her well, but I'm sure you know what I thought privately! With the best will in the world, there are some decisions we just can't make.

During my last year in Durham, I ran a series of workshops for the other dieters at the Rice House. These were essentially question-and-answer periods, in which patients were invited to ask me anything they liked.

Later I asked the medical staff what feedback they had received. The only complaints were from dieters who were outraged to hear me say they'd probably cheat. It was almost as if I had put a curse on them and had sentenced them to failure. They much preferred the fantasy that they were now completely in control, that having "decided" to diet, their problems with food were at an end.

I'm truly sorry, but in my opinion, that is nothing but wishful thinking. I can certainly understand that you might like it to be so, but it's important not to confuse high standards with unrealistic expectations.

Please note that I am certainly not counseling you to cheat. I am simply saying that it's likely that at some point you *will*. This is not to say, however, that you shouldn't avoid it when you can.

BEFORE YOU TAKE THE FIRST BITE . . .

In our society, wanting to eat usually has little to do with real hunger. I can think "Boy, I'm stuffed!" and "What can I eat?" at one and the same time. The desire to eat, almost for entertainment, can be powerful, even overwhelming.

But if you look at it more closely, staying on a diet isn't that hard—most of the time. The major part of the typical diet day causes little or no distress. We easily skip breakfast and eat minimally at lunch. But then comes nighttime—for most, the worst time—and the cravings begin. Food leaps into our minds, seizes control, and the battle is under way. Will we turn our thoughts into action, or will we be able to withstand the urge?

The main problem is that much as we sincerely want to lose weight, at that particular moment all we really want to do is eat. Indeed, it goes beyond wanting to eat, we're convinced that we *must*. This need, this compulsion, is a drive equal to none. We don't *want* to cooperate. We don't *want* to conquer the urge. What we crave is the "high," the release food can bring.

Because of our profound and conflicting emotions, this is a time of intense distress. We want to eat . . . yet we don't. We feel frantic . . . but excited, too. In this turbulent state of mind, any effort we make to control ourselves is bound to cause pain. What's important is to know that we can survive the anguish and win.

The truth is that food cravings usually pass very quickly. They can disappear in an instant, much the way they arrive. Sometimes diverting your mind for even a *second* is enough to do the trick.

Try to remember that you are not dealing with forever. All you have to handle is a few brief moments during the day. You just have to get through this (admittedly torturous) rough spot.

My advice is, THINK SMALL. Try to stave off the urge for just a minute or two. This will give your intellect time to impose itself over your desires. What you must do is apply your energy to diverting your thoughts from food. To continue focusing on food will ultimately lead to giving in.

All too often our bodies act almost automatically. A thought enters our minds and we act upon it at once. Like different passengers getting into a taxi, each passing, fleeting thought can command our bodies what to do.

But we do have alternatives, and indeed, this tendency to act automatically must be fought. Our mind may inform us that we really feel like eating, but our arm does not have to reach out for food.

The trick is to remove your attention from food and place it on any of the myriad other things life has to offer. This requires a great deal of effort, but you *can* cut down on binging by becoming involved with something else.

Substitution

I suggest that you pick a time when you are feeling positive, then sit down and make a list of all the things you like to do. Include activities that take as long as several hours (like shopping or going to a movie). Add activities that take only a minute or two (watching the sun set or patting your dog).

Your choices may include creative pursuits, such as handicrafts or woodworking. Or they may call for being a spectator, like watching TV or going to a ball game. Some may be sociable in nature and depend on the participation of others. Still other activities may require solitude.

Consult this list whenever you feel like binging, then force yourself to pick one activity—your choice—and do it before you allow yourself to eat. Don't be a hero. Take on some manageable unit of time. *Anything* you do will be exercising some control.

Place one copy of this list on the door of your refrigerator. If you've made it that far into the kitchen, perhaps it will help avert a raid.

Keep a second copy in another convenient location in your home so that, ideally, you won't have to go into the kitchen at all.

Tuck still a third copy into your wallet, should the urge to eat strike when you're away from home.

Most likely, you'll be tempted to do different things at different times. What's important to remember is to select activities that you *enjoy*.

Diet experts often recommend that you take a walk, or do some other form of exercise, when confronted with the desire to eat. But unless exercise is a favorite activity of yours, this is unlikely to be suitable as substitute behavior.

Don't choose an alternate activity on the grounds that it is "good for you." What is important—indeed, crucial—is to pick something that you *like*. Replacing something that you love (like eating) with something you detest is obviously not going to work. For substitution to be effective you must select activities that appeal.

Below is a sampling from the activity list I drew up for myself. Perhaps some of the suggestions will be suitable for your list, as well.

Take a bath, especially one with luxurious bubbles and oils.

Shop.

Watch TV.

Visit friends, or invite them over. (No refreshments!)

Do crossword puzzles.

Do jigsaw puzzles.

Play cards, either in pairs or solitaire.

Read in the magazine section of the library. (This is a good place to meet new people, too!)

Go to an auction or a flea market.

Water your plants.

Hum a tune, preferably a love song. (The kind of emotions these songs often arouse can help you stay on the straight and narrow.)

Read fashion magazines. (See where you're heading!)

Give your scalp a finger massage—hard.

Jump rope or do stretching exercises.

Go to a movie or a play.

Go to a sporting event.

Listen to music on the radio or stereo.

Play with a pet. (These "furry sedatives" are great at helping you relax. Not only do they occupy your attention, they engage you emotionally as well.)

People-watch in a mall or in an outdoor café.

Call a friend.

Write a letter.

Visit the Y or a spa. Take a sauna or sit in the whirlpool. Relaxing and luxurious!

Play board games or video games.

In fact do *anything*—anything at all. The object is to turn your attention away from food. Think about the things that give you pleasure, then use them wisely to buy yourself time.

Make your list as long and comprehensive as you can. If your activities require props, such as a deck of cards or a crossword puzzle book, have them on hand in advance. You will find that these more productive activities will help curb your urge to eat. Essentially, what you're aiming at is finding alternate ways of feeling good.

Some Binge Battlers

Though I've found substitution and delay by far the most effective in discouraging binges, there are a few other techniques that I've used with success. You might want to try some or all of the following:

- Talk to yourself. Tell yourself the things that, deep down, you really know. Like: "Only the first few bites are really going to be enjoyable. When I eat compulsively, I hardly even *taste* what I'm eating." Or: "I know I'll be sorry." (Then give serious thought to the way you'll feel the next morning.) Or: "If I eat tonight, intending to start dieting again tomorrow, it won't be any easier for me. These moments of crisis are always going to come. If I don't eventually say 'No,' I will always be fat." You might even want to talk to yourself in the mirror at these times.
- Sleep it off. Since most diet difficulties begin after dinner, put them behind you and go to bed for the night. I used to pride myself on my ability to get by with very little sleep. Until I realized that "getting by" and living life with zest are two different things. Now I take Dr. Kempner's advice and aim for eight or more hours sleep a night. I feel well rested and I avoid some of the dieter's darkest hours. Missing Johnny Carson occasionally is a small price to pay.
- When I'm feeling fragile and think I may binge, I have often found it helpful to ask a friend for support. Usually the mere act of seeking help prevents me from eating. Somehow, just *telling* someone I'm in trouble brings relief from the inner pressure to eat. You're helped just by the knowledge that someone is there.
- Along the same lines, joining a self-help group like Overeaters Anonymous cannot hurt. It's a rare meeting when you don't come away with something of value. This organization, in which membership is free, does not

promote any particular regimen, and it is thus completely compatible with following the Rice Diet.

- I have found that reading something elevating can often be of help. By this, I mean a good self-help book, religious works, or some of the Overeaters Anonymous literature. Very often, such reading miraculously provides the one idea, the one sentence, that illuminates a problem and helps to see you through.

- In somewhat the same vein are meditation and prayer. Not for you, you say? Well, maybe not. Still, it beats me how people will try pills, injections, even surgery but reject spiritual sources for help with their weight. Prayer and meditation offer peace, tranquility, and a good opportunity for insight. Personally, I have found both to be invaluable aids.

WHAT TO DO WHILE CAUGHT IN THE GRIP OF A BINGE

Given that binging is inevitable, let's take a look at it in greater detail.

A binge is an episode of uncontrolled eating. Once under way, it is virtually impossible to stop. At that moment, nothing in the world matters to you but food. Your adrenaline is flowing, and heaven help anyone who tries to stand in your way. As for substitution and delay—to heck with them: You want to *eat!*

In my old days of binging, absolutely anything went. To avoid waiting (I just *couldn't)*, I'd eat foods frozen solid from the freezer, I'd eat meat raw, I'd eat foods right from the oven, so hot they burned my mouth. I'd eat foods that I hated. I'd eat foods furry with mold.

I would describe that kind of binging as a descent into hell. I always felt panicky and driven, terrified and out of control. Sometimes food acted as a pacifier, but it went too far—it deadened and numbed.

Indeed, one of the things that saddens me is that during my seven-year period of great obesity, I hardly ever enjoyed any of the food that I ate. It was always tainted with regret, panic, and self-recrimination.

Although you cannot eliminate your desire to eat, you can learn how to exercise a greater degree of control over how much damage you do. You can work on how much, how often, when, and what you eat. A binge may represent a battle that was lost, but there are individual little skirmishes within it that can be won. Ultimately, improved eating behaviors lead to greater overall control.

Because I find it hard, once started, to limit the quantity of food I eat, I have found it easier to alter the type of foods I select. If I'm going to eat a lot, I'd rather eat something not too destructive. Overdoing it with foods that are good for you is not nearly as damaging as overindulging with salty or sugary junk.

My foremost recommendation is to cheat exclusively with Rice Diet allowables. You will not believe the amount of Rice Diet food you can put away with only the tiniest gain.

I'll give you some examples. There was one night I ate an entire watermelon and fourteen nectarines—in addition to my meals, it goes without saying!—and gained only half a pound.

Another time I ate (besides meals) a package of figs, a package of prunes, a portion of squash mixed with rice, one chicken breast, three slices of bread, two eggs, and a bowl of oatmeal. And was up only three-quarters of a pound!

Recently, I binged on seven regular potatoes, four sweet potatoes, six eggs, a piece of bread, half a pound of mushrooms, and four cups of strawberries. Result? One pound up.

I don't understand it myself, but it seems that putting good food into your body, even in excessive amounts, just doesn't exact that high a price. You feel full faster, it's very quickly lost (lots of fiber and bulk), and, best of all, it greatly diminishes the degree of self-blame you feel.

When I eat huge amounts of Rice Diet foods, I may

feel stuffed and I may even put on a little weight, but I never hate myself the way I do when I eat foods that I know are bad for me. At least I've put nourishing food into my body. And far from feeling sick, most of the time I feel downright good! Binging on Rice Diet foods may still be binging, but it nonetheless represents a far greater degree of control.

If I'm cheating with allowables, fruit tastes sweet and delectable. But once I've upped my intake to include sugar, fruit seems tasteless and bland. I can't appreciate it; I can hardly *taste* it. My palate now needs more stimulation to respond.

Worst of all is the difficulty of resuming the diet the next day. When I binge on allowables, it's not that hard to return to proper eating. In fact, usually I feel stuffed (all that bulk!) and am glad to cut down. But with sugar in my system, I feel cravings again the next day. My experience has been that sugar makes you want more sugar, and resuming a diet can elicit painful withdrawal symptoms, usually lasting a few days.

Eating properly is even more important than being thin. One good diet day won't change your weight significantly, but it will immediately make you feel better, both physically and emotionally. Eat properly and you feel "up." Eat destructively and you feel "down." And that's regardless of the number that appears on the scale.

Bad foods are your enemies and should, accordingly, be fought. If it's sweets, work at cutting them out, or at least cutting them down. Try to stop eating sweets entirely, just to see how long you can last. One day? Terrific? Now try for two! Keep working to extend the amount of time that you can go without. The fact that you may eat them again is not a sign of defeat. If you've avoided them for even a slightly longer period than before, that's a victory! Now try for *more*. To date, the longest I have gone without sweets is two months. Not perfect, but not bad.

Your objective is not to eliminate binging entirely—why keep knocking your head against a wall? But *do* try to accomplish something profitable with a binge. Try to wrest just one element of victory out of what seems like total defeat.

Did you eat the whole thing but manage to leave one bite? That's a victory! Did you go wild and eat 4000 calories, but not the 5000 you usually put away? That's just great!

I can put away two pounds of nuts and raisins and tell myself I have triumphed! True, I ate a lot, but it was all natural and healthy food. To my mind, this represents genuine progress along my own particular path.

These days, I find myself leaning toward baked potatoes and corn on the cob, even better choices than dried fruit and nuts. True, my quantities can be outrageous, but my battle with behavior is slowly being won. I am learning more every day about how to handle food in my life. I can't take on all of my food compulsions at once, but I *can* improve on some areas, bit by bit.

To do this yourself, keep trying to work downward. First narrow your binges down to include only your favorite foods. Then start chipping away at these, always trying to move in the direction of fewer sweets, fewer salty foods, fewer chemicals.

Don't worry if you stay at one level for a while before being ready to move on. Keep your goal in mind and keep working toward it, but don't attempt to wipe the slate clean all at once. Just do what you can.

Never take on a step that sounds like torture to you—you won't be able to do it. Take on only what you're ready and willing to do, something you don't really mind doing all that much.

I don't feel at all uncomfortable with the fact that I sometimes cheat. In fact, I like knowing that this outlet is there for me occasionally. Of course, I'm more at peace when I'm not overeating, but I also savor the knowledge, tucked away in the back of my mind, that from time to time I will eat those foods I still love.

Moreover, knowing that another binge is definitely somewhere on the horizon, I don't feel the need to pack in everything I like now. Most dieters reason that because they're "going on a diet tomorrow" and therefore will "never, ever be eating these foods again," they should pack away as much as they can *now*, before the jail gate clangs shut. Knowing that you will, indeed, be eating your favorites again can help alleviate this drive.

Some dieters like to plan their binges ahead of time. Perhaps they have a party or a wedding to attend, and they decide in advance that on that particular occasion, they're going to eat. If you're a Group A dieter, this is probably a workable plan. For dieters in Groups B and C, however, I suspect it won't work.

It is obvious that people with severe food problems very frequently give in to the sudden desire to eat that seizes the mind and silences the will. They do not have enough control to choose to eat at the wedding *instead* of giving in to a binge. The binge is going to win out anyway. That being the case, if they pencil in additional eating occasions, on top of the usual binges, they are simply adding to the number of days they overindulge.

Given the choice, I find it more satisfying to eat when I genuinely feel like eating (the traditional binge), rather than at a party or wedding, when I'm eating simply because the food is there or because I know it will taste good.

However, this is a suggestion that may not be suitable for you. If you don't have binges that overwhelm you and insist on being satisfied, then you are in enough control to schedule your cheats. If you frequently succumb to your drives, however, you'd be wise to limit your binges to those times exclusively.

And please, *please*, be careful not to start interpreting a binge. The fact that you have overeaten does not mean that you are doomed, hopeless, or destined to stay overweight. In fact, it "means" nothing. It just *is*.

I'd like to tell you how Dr. Kempner helped me put a stop to my counterproductive reaction to a binge. I had been on the Rice Diet for five months at the time and had not yet had a really damaging binge. Of course, I had cheated—in fact, lots of times. But I hadn't yet indulged in one of those old-time extravaganzas, when I eat without stopping and end up feeling sick.

Then one night, out of nowhere, I drove to a shopping center and hit every fast-food joint in the place. Indeed, some I hit twice. I went from Italian to Chinese to all-American and back. I pigged out for two hours and ended up nauseous in bed.

The hard part wasn't the weight gain; it was the shock to my concept of myself. After five months on a pretty good diet, I had actually come to believe that I was no longer even capable of such self-destructive behavior.

Immediately I began interpreting what this surely must mean. I thought, "If I can still do this, what chance do I have? Why bother staying on the diet, when I'm obviously going to put it all back on again?"

I was sure that the binge made some significant statement about me and about my prospects, and given my interpretation, I was ready to fly home the next day.

The following morning, despondent, I went in to speak to Dr. Kempner. I told him what I had done and asked if there was any point in my continuing. His reply? "Don't be silly. Everyone does something stupid now and then."

This response is simple and obvious, but it truly electrified me. In a second, he had changed my entire perspective. Once again, I had been demanding all or nothing of myself. *Of course* everybody does something stupid every now and then! I had done something stupid—*but that was all it was*. It didn't "mean" anything, and it most certainly didn't foretell my future. It was a brief, limited episode of insanity—and that's all.

So the advice is not just from me; it's from the Impeccable Source himself. When you binge:

Eat it.

Enjoy it.

Forget it.

THEN GET ON WITH THE JOB!

How Can I Stop a Binge?

There are ways to stop a binge once it's started, or at least contain it to some extent. Different strategies work for me at different times, so I'll pass on a variety of approaches for you to try.

• When you're binging, intermittently ask yourself, "Does this taste good?" After that ask, "Am I really enjoying this?" If the answer to either of these questions is "No," try not to continue. If you can't stop eating entirely, at least move on to something that you like.

    I remember the time I was chomping away at something or other when I remembered to ask myself those questions. I didn't get past the first question, because, in fact, the item tasted pretty awful. It was something I had concocted with whatever odds and ends of ingredients were in the house, and the result would never find a place in any self-respecting cookbook. After I had ascertained that it was, indeed, rotten, I tried to improve it by pouring honey all over it. It still tasted rotten, only now it was sweeter and had even more calories! Hardly an improvement!

    I realized that it made no sense at all to work at making something taste good if it simply didn't. And it made even less sense to keep right on eating it, hating every bite.

    Having looked at it logically, I was able to stop. Sometimes just being sensible with yourself tips the balance.

• Along the same lines, work at acquiring an awareness of when you no longer need to eat. Keep testing the water of your appetite, so to speak. If you're still hungry, and still enjoying it, fine. If not, call it quits.

- Another effective technique is to make yourself stop eating—just briefly—and assign yourself something else to do. Tell yourself, "I'll listen to this song all the way through to the end, *then* I'll resume eating." Or make yourself count to fifty or wait a certain number of minutes. Always choose a time frame you know you can handle.

  This approach gives you a feeling of some degree of control in what is essentially a very uncontrolled situation. Occasionally, it will prevent you from continuing on the binge. At the very least, it shows some control, and it gives you something to build on. Perhaps next time you can listen through *two* songs or count to a *hundred*.

- When in the middle of a binge, never plan what you're going to eat next. Don't be biting into one item while its successor awaits its turn on the plate. Concentrate fully on what you're eating at present, and after you've finished, if you still want to eat, decide then what your next food choice will be.

  True, this means waiting a little while between "courses," instead of starting right in on the next food you plan to demolish. But *you can stand it*. It's another way of pushing yourself beyond your perceived limitations.

- Similarly, never start preparing, cooking, or even defrosting your next binge item until you've finished what you're on. You *can* tolerate a hiatus of just a few minutes—yes, even in the midst of the insanity of a binge.

- Don't overlook water as a means of hastening the end of a binge. Sometimes a drink of cold water is all you need to bring yourself to the point of feeling satisfied and ready to quit.

STRATEGIES FOR THE
DAY AFTER THE BINGE

A binge is an instant high, the perfect example of immediate gratification. Its aftermath, however, is something else again. Most binges are followed by depression, despair, and an engulfing self-hatred. You feel unlovable, unloving, and absorbed in your pain. Your energy is low, your concentration impaired.

These are bad times, very bad times; you're obsessed with the binge. But remember, your goal is to *lose weight*, not to be on the "perfect" diet. It is not necessary—it is not *possible*—for each and every diet day to be "good." It is enough if the majority of your days are pretty successful, because the end result of such "imperfect" dieting is that eventually you'll be thin.

All or Nothing = Nothing

Overweight people tend to see life in all or nothing terms. They want the perfect body, the perfect diet. Everything in life must be "just so."

Alas, if you have an all-or-nothing view, there is no choice—you *must* end up with nothing. This is obviously so, since "all" is impossible to achieve. If the only diet options you allow yourself are two extremes, then you're either rigidly on a diet or eating out of control.

No one achieves perfection, not in anything they undertake. Yet many dieters seem to believe that they should never make mistakes. Why demand flawlessness of yourself when it's impossible to achieve? There is simply no such thing as the Perfect Dieter, and the times that your diet is less than perfect can be educational if properly used.

Both good diet days and binges are steps on the road to being thin, and the successful dieter is the one who can absorb the occasional binge. Please accept this from the start, so you won't be devastated when you eat more than you should.

Learn to be reasonable in both your behavior and your expectations. Don't be self-critical or intolerant when you fall short of your ideals. After all, you're only human, and that's perfectly okay.

You don't have to diet perfectly, you just have to diet *consistently*. A binge can be contained, and you must continue on your way.

Guilt and Blame

Stop regarding a binge as the end of the world.

Stop punishing yourself for having food/diet/weight problems.

A binge does not call for endless regret or vicious attacks upon yourself. In fact, guilt is a pretty useless substitute for healthy self-improvement.

Self-blame comes from not having our demands for perfection met. Essentially, we punish ourselves for having shortcomings. I ask you, what could be a more ineffective way of helping yourself change? Self-blame diverts your energy into unconstructive channels. You focus on your failings, and, like picking at a sore, it makes things worse.

You undermine your efforts when you criticize yourself. Now, in addition to the weight gain, you have upset feelings to contend with. Why continue causing yourself this unnecessary grief?

It would be well and good to blame yourself if all that pain and turmoil helped, but experience has surely shown you that it only increases stress. Continual preoccupation with your failings interferes with daily functioning. Each minute you spend making yourself miserable could be far more profitably spent. Dumping on yourself only diminishes your resources. Face it, if self-punishment worked, we'd all be perfect by now.

If you consider yourself "bad" for eating, you'll be bothered and unhappy. And thinking ill of yourself leads to treating yourself poorly. After all, how can you hate yourself and still be wholeheartedly and enthusiastically good to yourself? Who do you go out of your way for, those you love or those you hate?

Realize that you may not be perfect, but that doesn't

mean you're bad. What is really called for here is a dose of love and understanding.

Talk to yourself lovingly, because we all need love—including you. You need understanding, not self-punishment. You need gentleness, not rebuke.

Stop wasting your time, the precious minutes of your life. Stop being obsessive about what you ate or how many calories you had. Wasn't it bad enough to have lived through that experience once? Why go over it and over it and over it again? When you re-create an unhappy moment, it's like living it anew. Think about that, and you'll see that it makes no sense at all.

You binged? Okay, now put it behind you. Not just in diet terms, but emotionally as well. By all means, allow yourself a brief and beneficial moment of regret. Then stop thinking about it, stop obsessing about your weight.

Realize that it doesn't matter if you have bad days—in fact, it doesn't even matter *how many* bad days you have. What matters is the proportion of good days to bad. What matters is your long-range commitment to your goal.

Learn from Your Lapses

It's easy, but unproductive, to get discouraged about a binge. Good judgment comes from experience, and experience comes from *poor* judgment, remember that!

Don't focus on your worthlessness; instead, think of constructive ways to change. Your attitude can make the difference; regard the binge as a chance to learn.

I suggest that you replace self-recrimination with self-observation. In the aftermath of a binge, don't judge or evaluate, just observe. At these times, there is a tendency to call ourselves names and to predict a future filled with doom. Cool observation, however, will pay bigger dividends.

For example, when I first started eating at home, after two years at the Rice House, I had many things to learn. I was on my own again, in a house full of food, faced with shopping, preparing, and eating by myself. So far, I had known only two ways of eating food: the out-of-control way I had done before I left for Durham and the formally structured way imposed by the Rice House meals. I knew nothing else, so I had many skills to learn.

For example, within days of being at home I found myself in eating behaviors that distressed me. I was standing up in the kitchen, eating directly out of pots. Or I was in such a rush to eat, I burned my mouth on too hot foods.

My first instinct was to judge myself and forecast defeat. "Look at me! I've obviously learned nothing at all. I'm still capable of this out-of-control behavior. I can't live the rest of my life at the Rice House. I'm going to get fat again."

But when I stopped pronouncing judgment long enough to simply observe my actions, I saw that, in truth, I *prefer* not to eat standing up because it's simply not as relaxing and enjoyable an experience for me. Moreover, I don't like eating scalding food because, well, because it *scalds* me!

Having recognized the truth in these two observations, it was easy for me to stop both behaviors, virtually at once. I didn't have to make "resolutions" to stop. I didn't have to police myself or enforce a set of "rules." I saw that I didn't like the results of these behaviors and I didn't want to continue them—why make myself miserable? So I stopped.

Day-After Diets

Because people who go off a diet usually tend to think they're "bad," they approach the day after a binge in a punitive frame of mind. Yes, sir, they're going to cut back to the point of starvation, they're going to compensate for that lapse by instituting even greater deprivation.

I'm sure you can see why this makes absolutely no sense.

If you're having a hard time on the diet, what could

possibly be gained by trying to make it even harder? No, this is the time to be even *easier* on yourself. To be punitive and harsh is to guarantee that you will fail.

What, then, *should* you do the day after a binge? There are several possible strategies. Which one you choose depends on your frame of mind.

Take it nice and easy. When you're having a generally hard time with the diet, drastic measures are the last thing to try. On days when you just can't handle a major restriction of food, let yourself eat all you need *of the foods you're allowed,* at meals only. Have ten items during the day, or twelve, or even more. Recognize that you're hurting and that to make it harder for yourself now will not help.

Fast. Dr. Kempner likes to tell post-binge dieters to "starve," and there are times when that is appropriate advice. For one thing, it feels good and reassuring to immediately resume control after a totally out-of-control episode. You know that you're back in the driver's seat—for now, at any rate!—and that puts anxiety to rest. Moreover, a fast usually undoes most, if not all, of whatever weight you gained during the binge.

I fast after a binge only under the following conditions:

1. If I'm not feeling generally fragile about the diet or about anything else in my life.
2. If the binge took place late at night. If I was eating until two or three o'clock in the morning, I'll probably wake up still feeling stuffed. I'll feel nauseous just thinking about food. This feeling can last a good part of the day, which makes it possible for me to see a fast through.
3. If I can sleep in late the day following a binge. If it's a normal working day and I have to be up early, I know I have too long a day ahead of me to tolerate a fast. But if it's, say, a weekend, I know I can sleep

in pretty late. By the time I wake up, a good part of the day is over and a fast can make sense.

DO NOT CONSIDER FASTING IF IT'S GOING TO BE A STRUGGLE. Never assign yourself a difficult battle the day after a binge. You're too fragile; and worse, you risk another day of binging if you make resolutions you can't keep.

Have a strict diet day. Like fasting, this is a suitable suggestion only for those who are feeling more or less ready to resume a very restricted diet. To knock off quickly the weight that you gained, you might try one of the following for just one day:

Eat only five fruits (your choice) all day.

Go back to a Phase I day and have the usual rice and fruit.

Have one apple all day.

Have 5 to 6 grapes *only* at each of your three meals.

Try one of the diets recommended for plateaus (see pages 140–141.

Use a moderate approach. Halfway between the radical fast and the nice and easy day is the moderate approach, the one I most often use. What I do is . . . nothing. I stay at the phase I am on and have a regular Rice Diet day. The binge is not regarded as *breaking* the diet but is, rather, absorbed, and seen simply as *part* of the diet.

So there's no one right answer. Each binge requires its own assessment and prescription the morning after. Take a nonjudgmental look at the situation and decide for yourself the best approach.

And remember, the right choice is not the diet that will

knock the weight off the quickest. The only suitable choice is the diet *that you can do.*

I consider the day after a binge to be the most critical time of all. It is imperative that you immediately establish some control. Perhaps it's impossible to stop a binge once it's been started, but it is not really all that hard to limit the binge to just one day. There is some struggle involved because a certain "food momentum" has been generated. But think of how much harder it will be to resume after two bad days, back to back.

You can reacquire the taste for junk food very quickly. Indeed, it will snowball into an avalanche if you allow yourself to become accustomed to it again. It takes only a few days of bad eating for your palate to become acclimated again to salty, spicy, and sugary foods.

Sometimes, of course, you'll be confronted with a longer period of difficulty. If one day does damage, and two is worse, then picture a week! But the technique remains the same. Try not to have two bad days in a row. When I have bad weeks, I usually manage to alternate a bad day with a good day. In other words, I manage to intersperse enough good days into the mess to maintain my weight and feel I retain a degree of control.

MISCELLANEOUS TIPS

- There are some interesting things to note about binging on the Rice Diet. For one, salty food may make your mouth burn the first time you eat it again. It will also make you very thirsty. Naturally, the unaccustomed combination of salt and water causes bloat, but you'll lose that at once if you resume the diet right away.

- When you binge, you'll feel better immediately if you start to do something constructive. Believe it or not, household chores are a good bet. Clean house, do a laundry load, sew clothes, wash the car. It is crucial at this time to do something productive. You start feeling better about yourself, and this creates a better frame of mind.

- Be honest with yourself about the binge, but don't mistake brutality for honesty. It's okay to say, "I overate," but never say, "I failed." Even worse is, "I'm such a pig!"
- Don't itemize, either to yourself or to others, all the foods you ate during your binge. Talking about them leads to visualizing them, which leads to craving them again.
- Ask yourself, "What would I say to someone *else* if she came to me with this problem?" How would you view it? What advice would you give? Looking at it this way helps mitigate your tendency to be harsh with yourself. It gives you a better perspective on what the real issues are.
- Never say things to or about yourself that you would consider mean or insensitive coming from someone else. We often say things to ourselves that human decency would never permit us to say to another person. Be gentle; don't be callous or hurtful with yourself. After a binge, you're a sad and needy person. Give yourself kindness, acceptance, and love.

CHAPTER FIFTEEN

Eating Out or with Others

RESTAURANTS, PARTIES, entertaining, feeding a family—all these are challenging situations for the serious dieter.

Happily, it is not very difficult to incorporate the Rice Diet into your regular routine—as long as you take responsibility for getting your dietary needs met *no matter what*.

I recall the Ricer who went shopping with a friend, and the friend insisted on dropping into an all-you-can-eat buffet.

"What could I do?" moaned the Ricer. "She was eating, and because of her, I ended up eating, too."

She then asked me what I would have done, to which I replied, "I wouldn't have gone in."

"I suppose I could have done that," she sighed, "but I'm afraid I'm just not there yet."

Well, no, lady, and you won't be "there" until you decide to be "there." Indeed, I wonder exactly what she was waiting for that would transport her "there" ("there," I assume, being the place where one can easily and without struggle pass up a buffet).

As Dr. Kempner says, "To accomplish anything, one must be a fanatic," and nowhere is this more true than in following a diet. To put it bluntly, it is entirely up to you. You *can* keep to your diet, wherever you are, but only if you take the responsibility for making that happen.

This section offers suggestions to help you deal with some potentially treacherous situations.

IN THE SUPERMARKET

- Most supermarkets today have low-calorie sections. Speak to your store manager about opening a salt-free section as well. And let manufacturers know that there is a sizable market for salt-free foods.
- I'll repeat this again because of its importance. Read labels carefully and avoid any foods that contain sodium.
- Keep as little food as possible in the house. It's better to shop more often than to have temptations at hand. A bonus is that you'll always have the freshest fruits and vegetables.
- Don't wander around the store. Go straight to the items you need. Avoid the aisles containing junk foods and sweets. Don't examine new products ''just out of curiosity.''
- If family members insist on having nonpermissible foods in the house, don't allow them to buy your favorite flavors and brands.
- Your children do not need the convenience foods and snacks they usually eat. In fact, the best thing you could do for them would be to keep only healthy foods in the house. Give them a better grounding in nutrition than you had.

IN THE KITCHEN

- Buy a vegetable steamer for the crispest, most nutrition-packed vegetables.
- Use Teflon-coated utensils and pots and pans, or one of the sodium-free vegetable sprays.
- Don't have foods in the house that you can't eat. There may even be some permissible foods that you shouldn't keep on hand because you are unable to stop until you have eaten them all. For example, I don't keep dried fruits in the house. I am allowed them, but my tendency is to overdo. If I really want them, I go out and buy

them. Keeping them out of the house means I don't indulge just because I love them and they're there.

- If you must have nonpermissible foods in the fridge, place them in the vegetable crisper so that at least you won't see them every time you open the door. This means, of course, that you must remove *your* food from the crisper and keep it on one of the regular shelves.

- There should be no food anywhere in the house except in the kitchen, and even there it should not be visible. Keep all food out of sight, even fruit. Let fruit ripen in cupboards if it's not ready for the fridge. Remember your susceptibility to food cues and avoid unnecessary temptations.

- If you cook for others, make simple meals that don't require you to spend much time in the kitchen.

- Never bake or cook foods that were your favorites before you began the diet. Pick alternatives that you're not particularly fond of.

- Never taste while cooking. You're not adding spices, so what is there to taste? Restrict your eating to meals. And yes, tasting is eating.

- Cook Rice Diet meals for everyone in the family, then have the others season and adjust their portions as they wish. Let them add their own cheese, butter, herbs, spices, sauces, etc.—preferably in the kitchen, not at the table. It should not be necessary for you to handle these additions at all.

- Have someone else prepare the family's meals as often as possible. And ask someone else to do the dishes, so that you can escape further contact with food after meals.

- Stay out of the kitchen unless it's absolutely necessary to be there. Don't read there, work there, or use the kitchen phone.

- Do your food preparation when your control is the greatest. For example, because I rarely have any appetite in the morning, that is the best time for me to prepare foods I will need later on in the day.

- If you have to prepare lunches, do it while another meal is cooking. That will reduce the total number of times that you have to be in the kitchen. Even better, have other family members prepare their own snacks and lunches.

FRIENDS AND FAMILY

- If you have children, tell them what you're doing and enlist their support. Children can often handle change more easily than a spouse, who sometimes fears that your loss of weight will mean a serious change in the status quo of the relationship.
- Your friends and family will either sabotage or support. If they sabotage, you'll have to take a look at that, possibly with the assistance of a counselor. If they're supportive, lucky you. But remember, even the best-intentioned friend will sometimes make a mistake or mishandle a situation. Just as you're learning to allow *yourself* to make mistakes, try to accept that others will make mistakes, too.
- If you have friends who frequently place you in difficult eating situations, arrange to meet them in a neutral place such as on a street corner, at a museum, etc., instead of in restaurants or coffee shops.
- Remember that what other people think and predict means absolutely nothing. The night before I left Montreal for Durham, my friends threw me a farewell dinner party. One friend kept remarking, "I don't know why we're doing this. She's never going to last. She'll be back in two weeks." Everyone was appalled; they were afraid his negativism would affect my resolve. But my resolve was independent of anyone else's thoughts. No one can make you either fail or be successful.

AT THE TABLE

- Don't serve family-style. Instead, portion out food in the kitchen. You'll thus avoid the temptation to reach for a second helping.

- After eating a small amount, stop for a few moments to see if there's anything you can do for someone else at the table. Does someone need the bread passed? Or a napkin? This is one way of reducing your concentration on food and acquiring a degree of control.
- If the situation permits, get up from the table as soon as you've finished eating.
- Have others clear the table and put away leftovers.

ENTERTAINING AT HOME

- Serve buffet-style. Eat before your guests arrive, and no one will even notice that you're not eating at the party.
- Don't serve any of your favorites.
- Serve raw vegetables with your dip, instead of crackers or chips. If you're at Maintenance, you can make an excellent dip with plain yogurt. Experiment with permissible condiments for a taste that you like. My experience has been that today's guests prefer lighter fare.
- Try wine as a frying substitute for oil. The heat evaporates the alcohol, which contains most of the calories. What's left is flavor. Use regular table wine, not dessert or cooking wines, which contain a lot of sodium.
- Give all leftovers to your guests. They'll be delighted, and you will be safe.

AT THE OFFICE

- Since working people need fast, ready-to-eat lunches, your best bet is to take your own lunch to work with you. This is the easiest way to retain control over what you eat during the day. I think you will find, too, that a healthy Rice Diet lunch will help you cope more effectively with the various pressures at work.
- See if you can get your company cafeteria to start offering Rice Diet meals. And watch for less time lost due to illness!
- If your job calls for you to eat lunch out often, find a

nearby restaurant that will accommodate your requests, and frequent it regularly. It is my hope that as a result of this book, restaurants will start offering the option of Rice Diet meals to their patrons.

WHEN YOU'RE INVITED TO SOMEONE'S HOUSE FOR DINNER OR A PARTY

- Unless it's a sit-down dinner, eat before you go.
- Don't sit near the food placed out for guests.
- If you've eaten before going, don't go over to look at the refreshment table. After all, what's the point of looking at food if you seriously don't intend to eat it? You are simply exposing yourself to an unnecessary risk.
- If a buffet is being served and you do plan to eat, pass up the foods you're familiar with and limit yourself to the unusual ones that are worth spending calories on. Take tiny portions of the foods you find interesting, then go back for a regular portion of the one or two you liked best. That way, you get to taste everything of interest, but you don't end up eating more than you really want.
- If it's a sit-down dinner and you know the hostess well, you should feel comfortable phoning in advance and making special requests or asking if you can bring your own food. It isn't hard for a hostess to adapt almost any menu to your needs. Instead of having to do *more* for you, she is, in fact, being asked to do *less,* such as taking a portion of salad out of the bowl for you before she adds the dressing, or cooking a plain piece of chicken or fish separately, without the sauce.

  I hope that with the appearance of this book hostesses will know what Ricers can eat and will willingly provide simple Rice Diet meals to their guests, if they ask. Some of the items that lend themselves well to entertaining are baked fish or chicken, baked potato, salads, fruit salad or juice, rice, and omelets.
- Do not give in to a hostess's pressure to eat. Your no must be firm. I consider it immoral to pressure someone

with a weight problem to eat. You are certainly not harming your hostess by not eating her food, and you *are* harming yourself if you succumb to pressure and eat. Remember, there is always *some* eating occasion on the horizon, and if you don't learn to make your refusal stick, you're pretty much done for.

- Bring a dish to contribute to the party—something that you can eat.
- Dawdle over your food. Concentrate on the conversation, rather than the food.
- If anyone comments on your small intake, and you prefer not to talk about your diet, simply say that you're not very hungry today or that you're so full you couldn't eat another bite.

I personally prefer the straightforward approach, and I readily tell people why I'm keeping an eye on how much I eat. I do not see what is shameful about being on a diet. I'm *proud* that I try not to bend to temptation and whim.

- Drinks stimulate your appetite, and they are not on the diet until Maintenance. You should especially avoid mixers, which contain high proportions of sodium.
- If you do take a drink, dilute it with Perrier or sodium-free seltzer water.
- Bring a bottle of low-sodium wine to your hostess. You'll be taking care of a social obligation at the same time you are assuring that there will be something on hand for you to drink.

RESTAURANTS
Selecting the Restaurant

- Choose restaurants you know and can trust to prepare food to your specifications.
- Look for restaurants that offer a wide variety of food. You're more likely to find something you can order there.
- Go to restaurants where food is prepared to order. Phone

ahead to make sure this is the case. Otherwise, you will not be able to avoid salty preparations.

- If you know you're going to a specific, unfamiliar restaurant, call in advance to explain that you're on a diet and ask what accommodations can be made to meet your needs. Do not call during mealtimes, when the staff is rushed. About three in the afternoon is probably the best time.
- If you go to one particular restaurant frequently, have a discussion with the manager. Explain your needs and enlist the restaurant's cooperation.
- The best restaurant choices for acceptable meals are fish houses, Oriental restaurants (lots of steamed vegetables and rice), and vegetarian restaurants. In truth, you can find something permissible almost anywhere. The only occasion I had a hard time was in a Lebanese restaurant where the only acceptable food on the menu was fresh strawberries. So I ordered three bowls of strawberries and that was dinner!
- Restaurants with salad bars can be good choices. These range from fast-food outlets to the most elegant eateries. Ascertain if the salad greens have been sprayed with a sodium compound to retain color. If so, either skip them or choose to eat somewhere else.

  The following fast-food chains claim they do not treat their salad bars with any sodium compounds: Arby's, Burger King, Pizza Hut. Claiming the same are Bonanza, Sizzler Steak House, and Wendy's—and these three offer plain baked potatoes as well.

  Some salad bars also include fresh or canned fruit, both of which are acceptable on the diet.
- Avoid all-you-can-eat buffets, for obvious reasons. Not only are they laden with foods that will tempt you, but the issue will be further complicated by your desire to get your money's worth.

Deciding What to Order

- You know what you can have. If possible, avoid reading the menu altogether. Certainly pass over the dessert section.
- If you can, order first, then occupy yourself. You're too vulnerable to food cues to listen to others order foods you can't have.
- If you want a drink, a Perrier is your best bet.
- Fruit juice or fruit salad (even with sugar) makes a suitable appetizer. Of course, a fruit plate is a good main selection too, if you tell the waitress to omit the usual yogurt, sherbet, or cottage cheese accompaniment.
- Order à la carte, not complete meals. It is better to pay more and eat less. Money is not the issue here—your diet is. Consider ordering two appetizers and a salad, or an appetizer, a salad, and a baked potato. You can easily make a satisfying meal without ordering anything from the main course section.
- Order foods that are stir-fried without oil, or poached, steamed, or roasted.
- Order gravies, sauces, and dressings on the side—and leave them there. Ask for lemon wedges if you wish.
- Whatever vegetables are available in fancy preparations should be available plain as well. Ask your waiter. And when ordering a baked potato, be sure to specify "plain."
- At salad bars, don't eat canned or pickled items. Choose nothing in sauces or dressings, and use only lemon juice and sodium-free sweetener to flavor your food. (You'd better bring a few packets of sodium-free sweetener with you, in case the restaurant stocks only the other kind.)

Getting What You Want

A United States senator was a recent guest at the Rice House. I overheard him worrying aloud about how to get what he wanted when obliged to eat out. This man, who has a powerful influence on our nation's legislature, was concerned about getting a waiter to heed his commands!

The best way to get exactly what you want in a restaurant is to accept nothing else. Be *very* specific about what you want when you order. Speak confidently and without fear—after all, *you* are the customer. Order slowly and clearly, and make a point of repeating your order twice. If necessary, have the waiter repeat your instructions back to you. Be firm and let him know that your food *must* be prepared as you order it or you will be forced to send it back. And *do* send it back if you have to.

I carry my "before" picture with me to restaurants, and if necessary, I show it to the waiter to explain—most graphically—why my food must be prepared *exactly* as I order it.

MISCELLANEOUS

- Eating breakfast out is easy. Many typical breakfast items are acceptable on this diet, such as fresh or canned fruit, prunes, oatmeal, toast, eggs, juice, etc.
- In restaurants, have the waiter take your plate away as soon as you have stopped eating.
- If you're having a hard time coping with the display of tempting foods, excuse yourself and go to the washroom until you have regained your calm.
- If you're traveling by plane, call ahead and ask for a vegetarian or low-cal meal, salt-free. Another alternative is to bring along your own.

I hope that this book will help encourage a demand for airlines to offer Rice Diet meals. I would be thrilled to think this book could profoundly and permanently affect the eating habits of all North Americans.

CHAPTER SIXTEEN

Cosmetic Surgery?

IN A DIET community like Durham, where many lose 100 pounds or more, there is a great deal of interest in what plastic surgery has to offer. Here are some of the questions I am most frequently asked.

WILL I NEED PLASTIC SURGERY AFTER LOSING WEIGHT?

For the vast majority, there will be absolutely no need for cosmetic surgery after losing weight on the Rice Diet. On the contrary, your skin will be firm and resilient, and you will look as if you never had a weight problem in your life.

The only ones likely to be interested in some kind of surgical procedure after dieting are the following:

Those who do not exercise while losing weight. Exercise tones muscles so that they take up the slack left by the weight you are losing. Failure to exercise may mean that your skin will not fit your skeleton tightly and instead will hang down as flab.

Those who lose a very significant amount of weight, say, upward of 100 pounds. Like a blown-up balloon, an overweight person shows few wrinkles. But just like a balloon when you let the air out, as the weight comes off, wrinkles and folds can appear.

Those who lose a large amount of weight after the age of forty or so. At this point in life, your skin has a diminished capacity to shrink back to size.

WHEN IS THE BEST TIME
TO GET THE WORK DONE?

You should not have any plastic surgery performed until after you have reached goal weight and stayed there for six months to a year. There is a very real temptation to rush in and get the work done too soon, especially since many surgeons are willing to do it when you're within 25 pounds or so of your goal weight.

I believe it is a mistake to give in to this, and one that you will regret. Your flesh moves and shifts, even months after you have lost weight. If you have the surgery done too soon, you are likely to end up with pleats, folds, and bags that could have been avoided by waiting.

Only when you're at goal can you know for sure what needs to be done. If your surgeon is not working with your final-version body, how can he or she make the best decisions, not to mention incisions? My recommendation is: Be patient, and get the job done right.

WILL THE RICE DIET LEAVE ME IN
A SUITABLE STATE FOR SURGERY?

My dear, you'll be in the best possible state! Dr. Verne C. Lanier, Jr., Clinical Associate Professor of Plastic Surgery at Duke University, notes that Rice Diet patients show no indication of the protein depletion that sometimes accompanies drastic weight-loss programs. In his practice, he has observed that the condition of the skin of Rice Diet patients promotes excellent healing of tissue, since there is no depletion of essential vitamins and proteins.

WHAT CAN I DO WHILE DIETING TO GET MYSELF IN THE BEST CONDITION FOR SURGERY?

Dr. Lanier suggests the following:

Avoid the sun. Don't lie out tanning yourself to the point where your skin becomes dried out and leathery. This makes skin much harder to work with and can result in a less successful outcome. Wear a hat and a strong sun block at all times.

Don't smoke. Smoking causes permanent skin damage because of its chemical interactions with the skin. Since smoking decreases circulation, there is also a 30 percent higher risk of complications during surgery if you smoke. Nicotine causes your arteries to constrict, stopping blood flow—and blood flow is necessary in order to have viable tissue.

Exercise. Exercise is excellent for good, healthy skin. Just the opposite of smoking, exercise increases circulation. Your body warms up, and blood is brought to the surface of the skin.

Watch your hygiene. As you lose weight, you may need to bathe more frequently and keep your skin dry with powder. This eliminates bacteria and minimizes the likelihood of infection.

WILL I LOSE WEIGHT BY HAVING SURGERY?

Patients sometimes expect pounds to fall off as surplus flesh is removed. Alas, you cannot count on this. Although you may lose a pound or two, plastic surgery should be regarded strictly as body contouring, not as a means of losing significant amounts of weight.

WHAT CAN YOU TELL ME ABOUT A FACE-LIFT?

Well, for one thing, be sure that you need it before deciding to get it done. Sometimes your face starts to look gaunt while you are losing weight. This can deter people from losing all that they need to lose. Fearing a haggard look, they stop dieting before they reach goal.

This gaunt appearance, I assure you, is most often temporary. Time and again, I have seen dieters look gaunt—briefly—and within weeks their faces fill out again. When you're overweight, the elastic fibers in your skin are overstretched, and it takes time for them to contract and pull your skin back up again. This is another good reason for waiting at least six months after losing weight before deciding on surgery.

WHAT HAPPENS IF I REGAIN MY WEIGHT AFTER SURGERY?

A darned good question, and the best argument yet for waiting six months to a year before getting the work done.

From what I understand, weight gained post-surgery is even more unattractive than it originally was. Apparently, it comes on in bunches and clumps, making you look a little like the Michelin tire man.

No one can ever safely say, "I'm never going to put that weight back on again," but you should be pretty confident about your ability to keep it off before even considering plastic surgery on your body.

HOW DO YOU PERSONALLY FEEL ABOUT PLASTIC SURGERY?

Plastic surgery, competently performed, can result in many gratifying years of looking more youthful and attractive.

I believe that we're lucky to be living at a time when

such miraculous procedures are available to us. If your appearance is important to you, why not look the best you can?

Moreover, I consider the price to be more than reasonable, considering what it "buys." You can easily spend as much on a one-week vacation and have nothing at all long-term to show for it.

I opted for surgery, and I'm glad that I did.

CHAPTER SEVENTEEN

Beyond Weight Loss

DO YOU FEEL 100 percent terrific?

No? Then I'm talking to *you—all* of you, not just the overweight.

Because of my particular experience, the focus of this book has been on reducing. But it would be shortchanging the Rice Diet to leave it at that. I believe that *everyone* could benefit from eating the Rice Diet way.

In my opinion, the Rice Diet is the state of the art in human nutrition. It is exactly the way nature intended us to eat. Every species on earth has all the sustenance it requires available in pure and natural form. Why would nature have provided differently for man? True, we have the ability to mix and match our foods, but that doesn't mean it's a wise thing for us to do.

There is increasing evidence that everything from mental illness to cancer has some connection to faulty nutrition. Let's take a look at what some of these studies show.

FIRST, THE BAD NEWS

- According to the 1976 *Congressional Record*, six of the ten leading causes of death in this country are diet related.
- The same source says that one-third of the country's population is overweight to a degree that life expectancy is diminished.
- According to the *U.N. Statistical Yearbook*, the United States is twentieth in life expectancy among the world's nations, a shocking statistic. This country of wealth, education, and plenty lags behind less fortunate nations in

assuring its citizens long life and good health. This should not and need not be true.

- As much as 60 percent of the cancers in women and 40 percent of the cancers in men have been attributed to dietary factors. This suggests that more lives could be saved by the Rice Diet than by any specific cure for cancer.
- In 1984, a Public Health Service test showed that 50 percent of our students failed drills aimed at measuring overall fitness and health.
- Studies show that overweight people are more likely to have accidents. They are also more vulnerable to the effects of contaminants and air pollution.
- The mammals closest to us, apes and monkeys, are disease-free when they eat their normal, natural diet. Fed a typical American diet, they develop the same degenerative diseases that humans do.
- Degenerative diseases kill three times as many people as cancer does, seven times as many as accidents. They also are responsible for more chronic invalids. In the forty-five years since Dr. Kempner developed the Rice Diet, many other medical options have been developed to counteract the same degenerative diseases. Today's patient can opt for a coronary bypass (or two or three), a kidney transplant, or insulin injections. Surely healthy eating is preferable to such drastic interventions!

There are also the psychological effects of improper nutrition. It is generally accepted that the mind affects the body, but it is equally true that the body can affect the mind. If you have a toothache, for example, it will affect your psychological state, as well.

Some think that all of the above are unavoidable aspects of modern-day life. They are not; they're aberrations. Mental and physical problems are not "the norm" and "to be expected." You don't have to be depressed or have a variety of aches and pains. Indeed, you have every right to expect to feel just great.

Implementing the Rice Diet would dramatically affect this nation's health. Certainly we cannot continue to eat the way we do and flourish. If we insist on making it hard for our bodies, our bodies can make it very hard for us.

NOW THE GOOD NEWS

The good news is that a different future is possible. As one who has lived in both worlds, let me tell you that life is both different and better when your eating is under control.

First and foremost, YOU WILL BE HAPPIER. You will look better and feel better. You will be able to love yourself more, and you will be more lovable to others. In *no* way will your life be worse thin than it was fat. Life thin *versus* life fat is a no-contest bout.

Everything around you must and will change. Yes, of course you'll still have problems, but a different set of problems. Life is never problem-free, but living it thin is unquestionably an improvement. Believe me, giving up food (remember, only the kind that harms you) is a small price to pay for everything you gain by being thin. Whether your life is presently good, bad, or indifferent, I promise you it will be *better* when you get to your ideal weight.

Physically, you can expect better skin, stronger hair and nails, fewer headaches, fewer cavities, and virtually no dental plaque. You will sleep well throughout the night and awake well rested and alert. Elimination will be both regular and comfortable. In other words, your body will work *exactly as it should.*

Equally important will be the improvement in your emotional state. Proper eating will bring you peace of mind, calmness, and mental equilibrium. Self-respect will replace self-pity and self-hatred. When your eating is under control, things seem possible, instead of hopeless. Whatever crops up in your life, you'll find yourself better able to cope.

Food, diet, and weight will be of greatly decreased importance. You'll have one less thing to worry about, and a major issue, at that. You'll have more energy, more power, more ability to profit from life.

As for your appearance, well, energy and vitality are the essence of beauty, and these the Rice Diet can deliver, along with a slim, trim shape.

We are definitely becoming smarter about nutrition. The "Lite" line of foods is the fastest-growing segment of the food industry. Even fast-food joints are offering more healthful fare. It's as if we are finally realizing that a life of devotion to food is simply not that rewarding.

With the country increasingly leaning toward natural foods, natural fabrics, etc., I believe that people are now ready to adopt a truly natural diet. The Rice Diet will give your body as little stress as possible, while providing it with all it needs.

Good food is your body's friend, just as bad food is its enemy. Your body does not like being fed junk food and chemicals, and it has numerous ways of telling you so. Proper nutrition pays short- and long-term dividends. Try it and see if it makes a difference in your life. What, may I ask, do you have to lose by trying?

For those wanting to lose weight, the Rice Diet offers a safe, scientific method of permanent weight control. It proves you do not have to jeopardize your health in order to be thin. Yes, it is severe, but it is also speedy and successful. If what you want is results, the Rice Diet will deliver. If what you want is an easy ride, sorry, but this ain't the one.

I have now experienced the Rice Diet at all levels—as an obese person, as a somewhat overweight person, and as an unquestionably thin person. At no time has it been anything but perfect for my needs.

Perhaps it isn't accurate to say that if I did it, anyone can. But there is nothing special about me—except, perhaps, that I was willing. Willing to listen, willing to learn, willing to acknowledge that there was a price to pay.

And the rewards are overwhelming. There are more advantages to being thin than I could possibly convey to you. Life is better and more interesting when you're at a normal weight. I promise you, being thin is all that you are hoping for—and more.

AND BEST OF ALL . . .

You will not miss your old ways of eating.

You will not miss the food.

Given time, the Rice Diet will make you sane about food and weight.

Why choose to live your life in your head, obsessing about *what* you eat, *how much* you eat, what you're *going* to eat, and worst of all, *why* you eat?

It's time to put all that aside.

It's time to lay this issue to rest.

It's time to DO IT.

APPENDIX

SODIUM CONTENT OF MAJOR CITY WATER SUPPLIES

Unless otherwise noted, 100 percent of each city's water supply was tested.

STATE AND CITY	MG. PER 8 OZ.	STATE AND CITY	MG. PER 8 OZ.
Alabama		Hartford	0.6
Birmingham	2.1	New Haven	0.9
Mobile	0.6		
Montgomery	12.7	**District of Columbia**	
		Washington, D.C.	2.1
Arizona		**Florida**	
Phoenix (74%)	25.0	Jacksonville	3.3
Tucson	10.4	Miami	4.0
		St. Petersburg	1.4
California		Tampa	2.0
Fresno	4.0		
Long Beach	29.3	**Georgia**	
Los Angeles	16.0	Atlanta	0.5
Oakland	2.8	Savannah	0.9
Sacramento (85%)	2.8		
San Diego (57%)	23.6	**Hawaii**	
San Francisco	1.0	Honolulu (57%)	9.6
San Jose (80%)	6.8		
		Illinois	
		Chicago	0.9
Colorado		Rockford	0.8
Denver	3.5		
		Indiana	
Connecticut		Evansville	3.0
Bridgeport	0.8	Fort Wayne	3.5

STATE AND CITY	MG. PER 8 OZ.	STATE AND CITY	MG. PER 8 OZ.
Gary	1.0	**Mississippi**	
Indianapolis	2.6	Jackson	0.8
South Bend (74%)	1.9		
		Missouri	
Iowa		Kansas City	8.9
Des Moines (75%)	7.8	St. Louis	5.2
		Nebraska	
Kansas		Lincoln	5.9
Kansas City	5.9	Omaha	15.3
Topeka	26.2		
Wichita	14.4	**New Jersey**	
		Jersey City	1.0
Kentucky		Newark	0.8
Louisville	6.1	Paterson	0.9
Louisiana		**New Mexico**	
Baton Rouge	17.7	Albuquerque	10.4
New Orleans	4.2		
Shreveport	5.6	**New York**	
		Albany	0.3
Maryland		Buffalo	2.2
Baltimore	0.8	New York City	1.4
		Rochester	1.4
Massachusetts		Syracuse	4.0
Boston	0.5	Yonkers	1.8
Springfield	0.6		
Worcester	0.7	**North Carolina**	
		Charlotte	0.9
Michigan		Greensboro	0.6
Detroit	0.9		
Flint	6.6	**Ohio**	
Grand Rapids	1.1	Akron	1.4
		Cincinnati	4.2
Minnesota		Cleveland	2.6
Minneapolis	1.4	Columbus	4.2
St. Paul (90%)	1.4	Dayton	4.0

STATE AND CITY	MG. PER 8 OZ.	STATE AND CITY	MG. PER 8 OZ.
Toledo	2.8	Amarillo	5.4
Youngstown	6.1	Austin	7.8
		Corpus Christi	14.6
Oklahoma		Dallas	9.2
Oklahoma City	19.8	El Paso (97%)	28.3
Tulsa	1.0	Fort Worth	4.7
		Houston (83%)	19.3
Oregon		Lubbock (82%)	10.4
Portland	0.2	San Antonio (unknown %)	1.8
Pennsylvania		**Utah**	
Erie	2.8	Salt Lake City (92%)	8.5
Philadelphia	1.4		
Pittsburgh	2.6	**Virginia**	
		Norfolk	2.1
Rhode Island		Richmond	0.08
Providence (92%)	0.7		
		Washington	
		Seattle	0.3
Tennessee		Spokane (77%)	0.7
Chattanooga	1.9	Tacoma (94%)	0.6
Memphis	2.6		
Nashville	0.09	**Wisconsin**	
		Madison	0.7
Texas		Milwaukee	0.9

Source: U.S. Geological Survey, "Public Water Supplies in the United States, 1962."

DR. WAYNE DYER'S
National Bestsellers